Financial Skills for Teachers

JEAN M HARRIS

Routledge
Taylor & Francis Group

LONDON AND NEW YORK

Professional Skills for Teachers series

Delegation Skills for Teachers, Jim Knight
Financial Skills for Teachers, Jean M Harris
Presentation Skills for Teachers, Jean M Harris
Team-building with Teachers, Judith Chivers
Time Management for Teachers, Ian Nelson

This practical series is aimed specifically at developing teachers' management skills. The books include activities and suggestions for things to do, to encourage the reader to think about their own needs and experiences. It will be helpful to have pen and paper handy to write down notes or ideas as you read.

First published 1996 by Kogan Page Limited

Published 2021 by Routledge
2 Park Square, Milton Park, Abingdon, Oxon OX14 4RN
605 Third Avenue, New York, NY 10017

Routledge is an imprint of the Taylor & Francis Group, an informa business

Copyright © 1996 Jean M Harris

Typeset by Northern Phototypesetting Co Ltd, Bolton

British Library Cataloguing in Publication Data

A CIP record for this book is available from the British Library.

ISBN 13: 978-0-7494-1811-3 (pbk)

Contents

Preface

The purpose of this book is to explain some of the basic concepts of finance and to suggest ways of helping classroom teachers and heads of department to manage their funds. While it will also be of use to more senior staff, it does not go in detail into the legal requirements for accounting and financial controls.

The first chapter describes the funding of schools and in general terms the role and responsibilities of Local Education Authorities (LEAs), governing bodies and head teachers. We believe it important that everyone involved in school finances, at whatever level, should understand this background.

Senior staff and governors who have greater responsibility for finances must also read the more detailed directives produced by their LEAs, the Department for Education and other relevant documents. Some references that may be useful are given at the end of this book.

CHAPTER I

Background To School Budgets

Financial responsibilities of LEAs

Spending on education is usually the largest single item of local authority budgets, accounting for as much as 58 per cent of the total budget.

Under the Local Management of Schools (LMS) schemes Local Education Authorities (LEAs) no longer have to exercise direct and detailed control over the bulk of spending in those schools with delegated budgets. But the LEA is ultimately responsible for making sure that LMS is effective in providing better education. The LMS scheme:

- determines total resources available to schools;
- decides on the scope of delegated finance within the framework of the 1988 Education Reform Act;
- establishes the basis for allocating resources to schools;
- operates sanctions when appropriate (this could include withdrawing delegation).

LEAs have four main financial responsibilities:

1. To decide on the total amount to be spent.
2. To produce a scheme of local management (including a formula).
3. To derive budget shares for all schools covered by its LMS scheme by using the formula.
4. To monitor the school's expenditure and take action where necessary.

The systems and procedures which each local authority uses to set its education budget will vary in detail, but there are parameters common to each authority. Each LEA has the power, and duty, to decide:

1. How much to spend each year in its revenue budget.
2. How much of this it needs to raise from local taxes.
3. How much of its total expenditure should be allocated to each service for which it is responsible.

These decisions are usually taken by a policy or resources committee, but in making its decisions it will consider:

- what expenditure various services require;
- level of grant expected from central government;
- possible penalties based on central government targets;
- expectations of public reaction to its local taxation plans;
- local factors (such as rising or falling pupil numbers).

Other, apparently unrelated, factors can also affect what can be spent on education as these will make demands on the overall budget for the area.

The Local Management Scheme

The 1988 Act requires each LEA to prepare a scheme of local management. The scheme must include two key requirements:

1. A way of deciding the amount of the education committee's budget which is allocated to each school. This is called the *formula* and the amount of money allocated to an individual school is called its *budget share*.
2. Delegation of authority to the governors of each school to decide how that school's budget share is allocated. While the head draws up the budget, the school governors have to approve that budget. The governors also agree the limits of delegation and the head is then able to incur expenditure within these delegated limits.

Determining the school budget share

Each LEA is required to produce an annual financial statement in accordance with the provisions of Section 42 of the Education Reform Act. This covers:

- the total general schools budget;
- the budget shares of all schools covered by the scheme with a national per capita share per pupil;
- the financial values appropriate to each formula factor in the LMS scheme;
- the allocation to each school by reference to each formula factor and background papers to enable each school to check that its share is correct.

Differences which arise between schools when national per capita rates are quoted can be attributed to a number of factors, some or all of which may apply to any one school, eg:

- number of pupils – cost per pupil;
- lump sum allowances;
- premises cost;
- attached units, eg nursery, special education.

From here it is up to the school and governors to decide how their budget is spent.

While each LEA can devise its own formula it is obliged to consult schools and other interested groups before it does so. LMS schemes have to be approved by the Secretary of State, and the formula will form part of each scheme, so it must also be approved. The Secretary of State has provided detailed guidance on what schemes are to contain and how the formula should be constructed. There are therefore many features common in all LEAs. This guidance also gives targets, probably the most important of these being that 80 per cent of the budget is to be delegated on the basis of pupil numbers (DES circular 7/91). Many LEAs plan to delegate higher percentages.

Monitoring schools' expenditure

Schools with delegated budgets have the authority to decide how to spend the budget share which they have been allocated.

There is some ambiguity over the role of the governors in the process of financial monitoring. Although the governors have the authority to decide how to spend the budget share, the money is not theirs, but the LEA's, ie, it is public money; so the LEA has a continuing duty which is not clearly defined.

However, the LEA does have the power to suspend the governing body if they believe that the governing body has been 'guilty of a substantial or persistent failure to comply with' any requirements applicable under the scheme or where the governing body is not managing its expenditure in a satisfactory manner.

Most LEAs have a computerized financial accounting system linked to schools. The schools produce monthly returns which are fed into the system, and in most cases schools will receive a print out from Central Finance. This is sent (on paper or electronically) to the schools so they can reconcile their accounts with the central system. It will also monitor expenditure and income against the budget on a monthly basis. We will look at budgets and accounting systems in more detail in later chapters.

Most LEAs use a computer package known as SIMS, but if this does not suit their needs they are free to choose an alternative.

The governing body

The governing body should control the running of the scheme in a qualifying school within its delegated budget. Subject to these conditions, the governors and the head will have freedom to use the resources in the school's budget according to the educational needs and priorities of their school. The implications of the Act are that the money is not delegated to the head and staff, but to the governing body.

So, the governors can spend the budget share any way they want so long as it is for the purposes and benefit of the school.

Deciding on expenditure

In many secondary schools the annual budget exceeds £1 million, and in very large schools could reach £2 million. To decide on how this money should be spent it is sensible to begin by constructing a framework for the decision making process. This framework could be of two kinds:

- a committee framework
- a policy framework.

The committee framework will vary from school to school – there is no one 'right' way. And frameworks which are adequate now may need developing and changing as time passes. The committee framework, however, should cover such aspects as:

1. How involved does the head need to be?
2. Who will do the day-to-day work?
3. Does the whole governing body need to be involved in all decisions?

The policy framework will need to cover such questions as:

1. What aspects of finance need to be phased over two or more years?
2. How far ahead do we need to plan?
3. What needs detailed planning each year?

This policy framework should be linked into the school's overall management plan which will outline the strategy for the school over an agreed period (usually two to five years). We will look at planning in more detail later.

The role of the head

Technically the 1988 Act does not give the head any formal legal powers relating to finance. Therefore, any power he or she has is that delegated by the governing body. This means that the amount of power and freedom will be based on the trust and working relationship between the head and governors.

In the best relationships the head should be responsible for preparing the draft expenditure in detail. This plan should cover the coming year and be in accordance with the management plan for the next two or three years. The financial plan will be reviewed and changed next year in the light of this year's experience – this is normal business practice.

This detailed draft is presented to the governing body for discussion and approval. The governors must ensure that the money is being used to enable the economic, efficient and effective use of the school's resources. Also the governing body must comply with any reasonable conditions made by the LEA and not incur any expenditure which the head believes to be inappropriate in relation to the school's curriculum.

Auditing

The Director of Finance of the local authority has responsibility to:

- secure proper financial management of all the authority's affairs;
- report the authority's income and expenditure each financial year;
- ensure that expenditure is lawful;
- maintain an internal audit service.

However, these responsibilities do not cover school funds – the governing body is responsible for ensuring that the school's budget is managed properly and for reporting any financial irregularities to the LEA. It must ensure that proper accounts are kept and send a copy of these to the Director of Finance.

Internal auditors (employed by the local authority) have very wide powers. They will visit schools regularly to inspect financial arrangements and records. Not only is this to identify and prevent fraud, but also to offer help and advice on systems and procedures.

External auditors work on behalf of the general public. They are employed by the Audit Commission and will visit schools only rarely, although they have the same access to records and explanations as internal auditors.

Reference materials from your LEA and elsewhere

All LEAs will have a manual or guide book on LMS and within this there will be a section on finance. This will give details of the legal obligations of the headteacher, staff and governors of the school within that authority. There are certain national regulations which must be applied to all schools under LMS and the LEA has the responsibility for ensuring that these are carried out.

In addition to these national and legal obligations there may be matters of detail which vary from one authority to the other. For this reason it is important that the responsible senior staff and governors make sure they obtain these documents and study them in detail. In addition, Croners' *School Governors' Manual* is a very useful reference book.

Most local authorities will give support and advice on financial matters, and some will provide training. Where possible you should take advantage of this local support as it will provide information particularly relevant to your LEA and tailored to your school's needs. The type of support provided might include:

- IT support and financial management software systems
- financial consultancy
- a personal school finance officer
- a help desk.

LEAs have the right to withdraw financial delegation from schools where there is substantial or persistent failure to comply with required procedures or mismanagement of funds.

Schools cannot plan for deficit – they must 'live within their means' and budget for the money they have. We will look at financial controls in Chapter 7.

Income

It is possible that your school is able to generate income through the provision of goods and services. This is normally acceptable but must be administered correctly. The Ofsted guidelines (*Keeping Your Balance*) state:

Income is vulnerable and the income collection system should meet the following objectives, namely that:

- all income including VAT due to the school is identified;
- all collections are receipted and banked promptly and completely;
- the accounting records and debtors' accounts are properly and promptly updated.

Where possible schools should obtain money in advance of the supply of goods or services as it improves the school's cash flow and also avoids the time and cost of administering debts.

There are standards laid down for this and if your school is generating income of any sort you must ensure that your school policy is aligned with the charging policy of the LEA.

Charging for school activities

The Education Reform Act 1988 introduced new provisions dealing with charges which may be made in maintained schools. The Department of Education and Science issued circular number 2/89 on 12 January 1989 commenting on these provisions.

Charges MAY NOT be made in the following instances:

- for admission to any maintained school during school hours for education (but for music tuition);
- for any materials, books, instruments or other equipment used in such education ('incidentals'); equipment for these purposes does not include clothing;
- outside school hours for education and associated incidents which are:
  - required as part of the syllabus for a public examination;
  - provided specifically to fulfil duties relating to the national curriculum or religious education;
- for transport provided to carry pupils between different parts of the school premises;
- examination entry fees for a public examination.

Charges MAY be made:

- for individual tuition in playing a musical instrument but *not* where:
  - required as part of any syllabus for a public examination;
  - provided specifically to fulfil duties relating to the national curriculum or religious education;

(Parents must first agree to the particular provision being made and are responsible for the charge if made.)

- a 'residential trip'.

Charges may not exceed cost.

The Act specifically leaves open the opportunity to invite voluntary contributions for the benefit of the school or any school activities.

School trading

If your school 'trades' it must comply with the Trade Descriptions Act

1968. The most important aspect of this is that it is an offence to issue false or misleading descriptions of goods, services, accommodation or facilities provided. In particular, the Act refers to:

(i)   the provision of any services, accommodation or facilities;
(ii)   the nature of any services, accommodation or facilities provided;
(iii) the time at which, manner in which or persons by whom any services, accommodation or facilities are so provided;
(iv)   the examination, approval or evaluation by any person of any services, accommodation or facilities so provided; or
(v)   the location of amenities of any accommodation so provided.

Private schools offering their tuition in return for the payment of fees come within the scope of the Act. It would be wise to exercise prudence in brochures and newsletters issued to parents, prospective parents and others enquiring about these schools. If statements made in advance of the circumstances to which they refer are subsequently found to be inaccurate, they would not contravene the terms of the Act if the details were accurate at the time the statement was made. An example might be an alteration of the planned curriculum caused by late changes of staff. Advice may be sought from the trading standards department of the local authority.

VAT

Value Added Tax (VAT) is administered by HM Customs and Excise. They may consider any activity which generates income as a business and you could be liable to register for VAT. You can obtain free advice from your local VAT office, or obtain current leaflets from the VAT Central Unit – the address is given in the References.

In business, VAT is collected at all stages of the production or distribution of goods. The final tax is borne by the consumer, but during the process the supplier will have to charge VAT (output tax) although the recipient may be able to claim it back (if they are registered for VAT).

Some goods or services are exempt from VAT, and some items are zero rated. Both these mean that no output tax is chargeable on the supply. However, there are these important differences:

1. 'Zero-rated' supplies are technically taxable (although the rate of tax is nil, and the VAT charged on inputs relating to them can be reclaimed like other input tax).
2. A person who makes zero-rated supplies will generally be registered with Customs and Excise and make VAT returns. A person who makes only exempt supplies cannot register or make returns.

Most educational services, such as the following, are exempt:

1. The provision of education if it is provided by a school or university or it is of a kind provided by a school or university and is provided otherwise than for profit.
2. The supply of any goods or services incidental to the provision of any education included in 1 above.
3. The provision of any instruction supplementary to the provision of any education included in 1 above; but VAT may be chargeable on recreational activities provided by LEAs for adults.
4. The provision by a youth club of facilities to its 'members'.

VAT can be a complex issue and if you believe your school should be liable for VAT you should seek the advice of your LEA financial adviser.

Business gifts to schools

The 1991 budget introduced tax relief for gifts of equipment made on or after 19 March 1991 by businesses to schools or colleges. The tax relief applies to gifts by companies or unincorporated businesses of items of equipment which they use, manufacture or sell. 'Equipment' is broadly defined by the Treasury and includes books, computers and laboratory apparatus. If a school or college makes enough profits to be taxed, it can deduct the market value of these gifts from its taxable income.

Again if you are liable to pay tax (unlikely in the case of most educational establishments!) your LEA financial adviser will be able to guide you.

Voluntary funds

Voluntary funds often provide schools with a substantial additional source of finance. Although such funds are not public money the standards outlined in your LEA's documents are equally applicable. Parents and other benefactors are entitled to the same standards of stewardship for voluntary funds as for those provided by government or the local authority.

Summary

The LEA has a responsibility to produce a local management scheme which satisfies the criteria of the 1988 Act.

Under Local Management of Schools LEAs no longer have to exercise direct and detailed control over most spending with delegated budgets. The school controls this, under certain rules laid down by the Secretary of State, with the governors and headteacher being accountable for this expenditure.

The money is, technically, delegated to the governing body.

Schools have an obligation to maintain good financial practices and obtain value for money. The LEA has the authority to audit schools to check that this and other financial regulations are complied with.

Each LEA has its own detailed scheme and all those responsible for school finances must make sure they know the requirements that relate to their role.

CHAPTER 2

Basic Financial Concepts

In Chapter 1 we described the framework within which financing of schools takes place. We will now explain some of the basic concepts used in finance. Although some of these may not at first appear to be relevant to schools, it is still important that you understand them. They are the key concepts on which an understanding of financial control are built. Although you may not use them in your day-to-day school finances you may be involved in setting up businesses within school (a Young Enterprise Company for example).

Costs

These can be divided into:

- Fixed costs
- Variable costs
- Direct costs
- Indirect costs.

Fixed costs – *those such as rates, insurance and depreciation, which do not change with the amount or frequency of the goods and services provided*

When you are planning how much anything will really cost you must take account of these items, whether you produce one item or thousands. In the case of schools the fixed costs will normally be set by factors beyond the control of individual schools, certainly beyond the control of individual teachers.

Variable costs – *costs which change at different times*

In business these will vary as production volume or number of services change. In schools they will vary, for example, with the number of pupils. This will affect the number of staff, the amount of stationery used, the number of textbooks required and so on. These costs could also include power supplies (for light and heat).

Direct costs – *costs directly related to making a product or providing a service*

In business these could be the wages of labour working on the product or the costs of raw materials. In schools these will be the costs directly related to the number of pupils you have (eg, books and equipment).

Indirect costs – *costs not directly related to making the product or service*

In business this could be back-up staff (eg, personnel, wages clerks) and cost of running the office and insurance premiums. In schools much of this is borne by the LEA, but will include costs for power, administration, cleaning and so on.

Although four types of cost are identified, there is some overlap. The reason for identifying costs in these different ways is partly for accounting purposes and partly to enable the organization to work out the true cost of producing specific items. If you are selling a product it is important that you take into account all the costs involved, not just the more obvious direct costs. In running a school these costs will all need to be taken into account when planning your budgets.

Overheads

Costs essential to running the business – *they may or may not be directly related to the provision of a particular product or service*

This term has a similar meaning to indirect costs, but might include some items used directly in making the product or service. The important factor is that it includes all items which are necessary to run the business but are not directly related to producing the end product.

In a school, overheads would include: rates, utilities (power, heat, light, water), cleaning, maintenance, administration staff, telephone calls, equipment not used by pupils and so on.

ACTIVITY

In the first column below note which of the following are fixed costs and which are variable costs. In the second column note which are overheads and finally note which are direct or indirect costs.

	F/V	O Yes/No	D/I
Purchase of books			
Cleaning			
Buildings maintenance			
Rates			
Fuel			

Items which directly relate to the teaching of pupils are direct costs and most of these will vary with the number of pupils. So books are variable and direct but not overheads. Items which have to be paid, no matter if the use varies, are fixed, so rates would be fixed. These are also an 'overhead' and they are not directly related to the teaching work of the school. Fuel is variable and an overhead, and indirect to the work of the school. Cleaning and maintenance are overheads, but although normally paid on a fixed contract, ie are fixed costs, the amount of work required could depend on the usage of the building, so they could also be considered as variable. But they are indirect costs as they are not directly related to the teaching work of the school. Unfortunately, as you can see, the division of costs is not a simple matter!

Capital expenditure

Expenditure on fixed assets (see below)

This expenditure will vary from year to year depending on the items purchased.

Fixed assets

Items purchased and owned by the school

These are the means by which a company would earn its income. They will be used over many years. They are an 'asset' because they have a value to the organization, and 'fixed' because they are not for sale in the course of everyday business.

In a school this would include buildings, land, computers, furniture and large items of PE equipment but not disposable items or small items which might wear out or get lost easily.

Revenue

The money that the organization receives

In the case of a business this will be the income from its goods or services less any taxes. It could also include income from investments.

In the case of a school this may mean the income from any goods or services it supplies plus the money it is given by the government and local authority.

Depreciation

The way in which the reduction in the fixed value of an item is shown in the accounts

We all know that most items become less valuable as they get older, ie they 'depreciate', but in the case of businesses their assets are devalued in the accounts each year by an amount agreed by the Inland Revenue. This is a fixed percentage of the value and varies with the type of asset.

In the case of schools this tax-related depreciation is only of interest if the school is liable for tax. The 'real' effect of depreciation, ie when assets need replacing – is more likely to interest schools.

Profit

Revenue minus costs

This is the amount left over from the sale of goods or services after you have taken out all your expenditure. This might include costs for materials, labour, overheads, transport and so on.

Companies may state profit either 'before or after tax', this is before or after the payment of corporation tax and other taxes due to the Inland Revenue – not VAT.

In the case of LEA schools it is unlikely that they will make a profit. Although a school may generate an income, its expenditure will normally be equal to the income plus the revenue received. Any 'profit' will usually be spent on more equipment or facilities.

Break even

The situation when income = costs

Most business organizations want to do better than break even – they want to make a profit. But this is not always the case. Charities, for example, are not allowed to make a profit – to maintain their status as charities, they must spend everything they earn on the cause they are supporting, otherwise they may be liable for VAT and tax.

Schools are not allowed to make a loss (*deficit*), so a 'break even' situation is the one they would aim for, where any revenue or income is balanced by the expenditure on educating its pupils.

Reaching a break even is a very difficult balancing act, almost impossible to achieve on a short-term basis, but possible in the longer term with good financial management.

Summary

Costs are divided according to whether or not they vary with use, and are related directly to the provision of the product or service (ie teaching in schools). They are therefore *fixed* or *variable* and *direct* or *indirect*. Costs can also be considered as to whether or not they are essential to running the school or business, but not directly related to providing the product or service.

The way money is obtained or spent and how it is held in the business is also given specific terminology.

Details of the meaning of the terms covered in this chapter are included in the Glossary at the end of this book.

CHAPTER 3

What is a Budget?

Budget

A budget is the forecast of what you *expect* to spend.

If you are planning a major purchase (a new car, a new fitted kitchen, a holiday) you will probably think about what you can afford. You will look at your income (what you earn), your expenditure (what you spend) and see if there is any surplus or money left over. Then you will decide how much you can afford for your purchase. This is your *budget* for that item.

Let's see how this might look written down on paper.

100 Any Road
New Kitchen Budget

ITEM	COST (£)	
Furniture:		
floor units	1,500	
wall units	950	
worktop	750	
plinth and other fittings	450	
sink and taps	500	
Subtotal		4,150
Appliances:		
cooker hob	500	
oven	600	
cooker hood	450	
built-in fridge	400	
Subtotal		1,950
Work:		
rewire cooker point	50	
move outlet for		
washing m/c	60	
fit units	280	
Subtotal		390
Total		6,490

The things you have already allowed for in your budget are the essentials to get the job completed to the quality you want.

If you manage to buy some items cheaper than you budgeted for you will have money left over after the purchase, that is you will have surplus. You might, for example be able to put down some new floor covering or buy a new dishwasher. But you might be more sensible and choose to save this in case there are any extras to pay which you did not expect (such as plasterwork, plumbing parts or more wiring). This is your 'contingency'. If you have money left after all that you could still buy the extras.

If the job comes to more than you expect you will have *overspent* your budget; you have made a loss so owe money and have to find that from your future income.

A budget in an organization works in much the same way. You work out a plan of what you will need to spend to get the job done. You work out the costs as carefully as you can, but you may have to allow some extra for the unexpected – it is foolish to commit *all* the money you have without having some contingency for the unexpected.

Why is a school budget important?

The budget has a controlling influence over the whole cycle of school affairs. Budgetary control is a continuous process in which the school reviews and adjusts budgetary targets during the financial year. It also provides a mechanism to call budget holders to account.

Below is an example of a budget from one school department.

GREAT LONDON SCHOOL
Geography Department

	Last year budget	Last year actual	Proposed budget
MATERIALS			
Stationery	500	500	750
OHP supplies	180	195	200
TEXTBOOKS			
Atlases	270	300	–
Europe textbooks	360	390	–
Year 8 textbooks	–	–	585
OTHER EQUIPMENT			
Geology sets	250	250	–
Thermometers	–	–	80
Measuring tapes	–	–	60
Compasses	–	–	40
SERVICES			
Computer contract	200	200	210
Photocopying	150	175	175
Telephone	120	100	100
OTHER			
Field trips' transport	1,200	900	1,000
Contingencies	100	100	100
TOTALS	**£3,330**	**£3,110**	**£3,300**

This is a simplified budget and it covers only the items which are of interest to that particular department.

Items in the general schools budget

The general schools budget is the full provision made by the LEA for the education of all the registered pupils in its primary and secondary schools and units. It includes both the direct costs of the schools and the indirect costs of services used by the schools or attributable to them, such as central administration costs or premature retirement compensation.

Normally the general schools budget does not include provision for items such as:

- nursery schools
- special schools
- non-school activities like adult education
- non-maintained school fees
- careers service.

The direct costs of schools which are included in the general schools budget and which are delegated to schools may include salaries, wages, employers' National Insurance and superannuation contributions and other employee expenses for:

- teachers
- classroom assistants
- midday supervisors
- administrative and clerical staff
- technicians
- building services supervisors
- pianists
- other staff.

Premises costs:

- non-structural repairs
- grounds' maintenance
- energy
- rents and rates
- water
- sewerage
- furniture
- security
- cleaning.

Transport:

- travel and subsistence
- car allowances.

Supplies and services:

- books
- equipment
- examination fees
- printing and stationery
- telephones
- postage
- subsistence
- other goods and services.

These items are typical, but may vary in detail from one LEA to another. In addition a proportion of indirect costs may be delegated to schools. This might cover items such as some LEA administration and advisory services, educational social workers, school meals and school crossing patrols.

Allocating the budget

The process of allocating the budget should not simply be an incremental process from one year to the next but should reflect, in monetary terms, the school's aims and objectives within the available resources. As the school development plan may lead to changes in priorities for expenditure in successive years, the emphasis should be on the objectives that the school wants to achieve rather than on the monetary inputs. Otherwise the governing body will be unable to assess whether requests for expenditure are really needed in line with overall objectives. They must also be able to determine whether value for money is being obtained from the budget.

The planning process

As we have said above, the budget is closely linked to the planning process. It is essential that each school produces its strategic plans in short, medium and long term. The school should have a written statement of its aims and objectives in sufficient detail to provide the basis for constructing budget plans.

It is the role of the headteacher and governors to set the strategy for the school, normally in consultation with other members of staff.

This strategy will set the long-term aims and objectives for the school, and may include estimates for the main capital expenditure items.

From the strategic review the medium-term plan will be drawn up, with more details of expenditure which affects the whole school. Finally an annual plan will be drawn up with details of each department's budgets, capital expenditure, overhead and fixed costs, and expected income.

The governing body should establish formal procedures and timetables for planning the budget to ensure that all relevant factors are considered.

The details of how this is done will vary according to the local guidelines and the style of each school. A diagram of a typical budgeting process is given below.

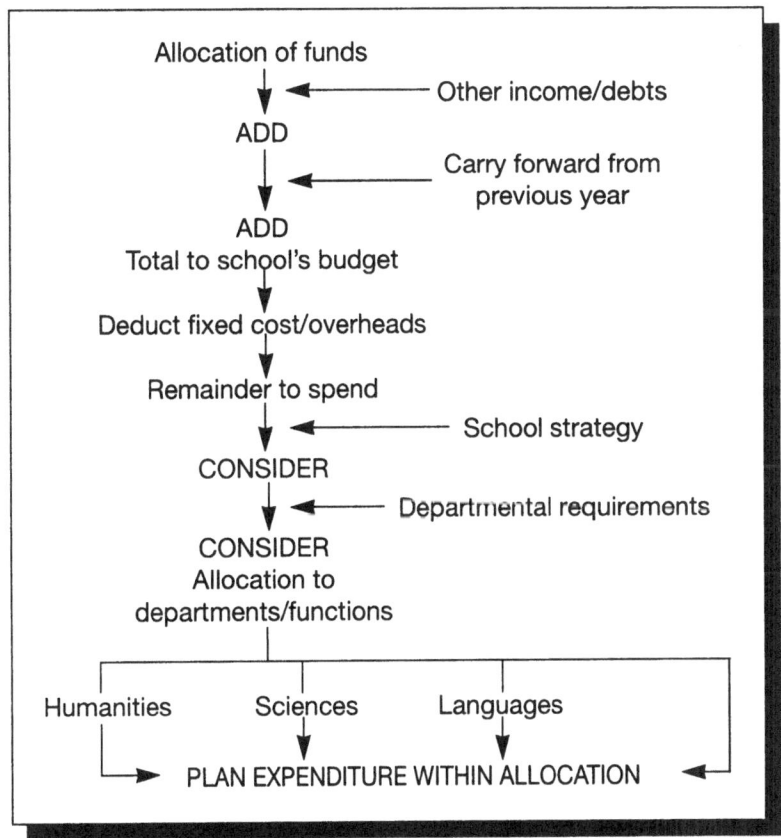

Details of budgeting are likely to be controlled by the financial committee, made up of the head, some governors and some staff.

The mechanics of budgeting

Total school's budget

The financial committee will need to begin by estimating the budget available. This could be from a number of sources:

1. The LEA – most LEAs provide indicative budget figures early in the calendar year; Section 42 statements giving final Figures must be published by 31 March.
2. The carry forward of surplus or deficit from the current financial year; final figures may not be available from the LEA for two to three months into the new financial year.
3. Lettings of premises.
4. Charges to pupils under the school's policy drawn up in accordance with the Education Reform Act 1988.

Some schools may have income from other sources, for example regular sponsorship or trading activities such as crèches, that they may wish to include within the budget. Most schools receive money from parent-teacher associations (PTAs) or similar bodies, which may be requested for specific items. To include PTA funds in budget plans is likely to be contentious and is probably best avoided. Moreover, any funds that must be earned (other than reliable and regular sources) are uncertain and it will generally not be wise to rely on these in producing the budget.

School strategy

The committee's next step is likely to be to estimate the cost of implementing each of the objectives in the school development plan. These are likely to include maintaining (or making changes to) current staffing levels. Staffing accounts for a very high proportion of costs and at first sight the governing body may have discretion over very limited areas of funding. In reality very few costs are fixed; a school must pay its rates but in most areas there are alternative ways of achieving school aims at different cost levels without necessarily compromising quality. In primary schools the committee is likely to obtain most of its information on which to base estimates of cost directly from the head. In most secondary schools and some larger primaries senior staff and the bursar, if applicable, may contribute information on different areas.

Detailed budgets

All the budget costs and estimates must be prepared in cash terms. So they must include realistic estimates for inflation. They must allow/plan to keep back 1–2 per cent of their budget for contingencies. This may not be easy but is essential for good management and to enable the school to cope effectively with the unexpected. For example, schools cannot expect additional funding to compensate for inflation.

The headteacher should prepare estimates of expenditure and income sufficiently in advance of each financial year to allow for consideration and approval by the governing body. Even if details of the school's funding have not been finalized it is important that the governing body considers spending priorities in the light of an estimated or indicative budget. There should be a clear, identifiable link between the school's annual budget and the school development plan.

Although the Section 42 statements published by LEAs set out the basis of calculation they are not a constraint on how the governing body may distribute funding across budget headings; the Section 42 statement may show premises-related factors but these need not be taken as an indication of the sum to be set aside for energy and maintenance.

Because LEAs are not required to publish Section 42 statements before 31 March the school's financial committee may be unable to produce a budget for approval by the full governing body until some weeks after the start of the financial year. It is important to recognize that budgeting is more of an art than a science, and that as the year progresses there will be changes to projected income and expenditure. The budget must be flexible enough to allow for this.

The school budget cannot show a deficit, so if the funds are lower than expected the committee will have to revise its budget. It may wish to consider factors such as:

- Could some expenditure be phased? For example, by spreading maintenance or the introduction of a new scheme over a longer

period, could the cost be spread over more than one year?
- Could some objectives be achieved by a different means costing less?
- Could contracts with suppliers be re-negotiated?
- Do you need to reassess your priorities and cut the least urgent? If this is to be done it must be handled sensitively to ensure that all concerned will still 'own' the revised plan.

Progress against the development plan and the performance against budget should be monitored by the head and governors regularly. We will look at recording financial information in the next chapter, as this is the basis for control which we will look at in Chapter 7.

Producing a budget

We showed an example of a simple budget earlier in this chapter, and with the 'kitchen' example we could have planned for what we would really like and then found ways to raise the money. Or we could have started with our budget and looked for what we could afford. Planning a school budget is usually a compromise between these two. But it is best if each year's budget is planned afresh – with reference to the school's development plan and taking account of past performance.

It is very tempting to look at last year's budget, add a percentage for inflation and put that forward. This is neither satisfactory or sensible. Each budget should be built up from scratch (companies call this *zero-based accounting*). In this way you examine every item in the budget and you have to justify why it is necessary and what it will cost.

The steps to building up a budget for a department form the next activity.

ACTIVITY

You are the head of department of your subject area (the one you are working in now).

Go through Steps 1–7 below. If you do not know the objectives for your department – find out now!

Compare your budget with the departmental budget that actually exists.

1. How do the school's aims affect my department? List them as key objectives.
2. What do I need to do to achieve these objectives?
3. What resources will I need? (Staff, equipment, other.)
4. What will this cost? (See Chapters 5 and 6.)
5. What is:
   (a) essential
   (b) nice to have
   (c) peripheral?
6. What is the 'essential' expenditure?
   What is the 'nice to have' expenditure?
   What is 'peripheral' expenditure?
7. Draw up your budget – remember to include allowance for inflation and contingency.

Summary

A budget is a forecast of what you expect to spend.

Each year the budget should be planned from a zero base to ensure that all items are justified and carefully costed.

The master budget for the whole school needs to take account of:

- general administration and support needs
- departmental needs
- the school's aims and objectives
- funds available.

Budgeting is part of the overall planning process as shown below.

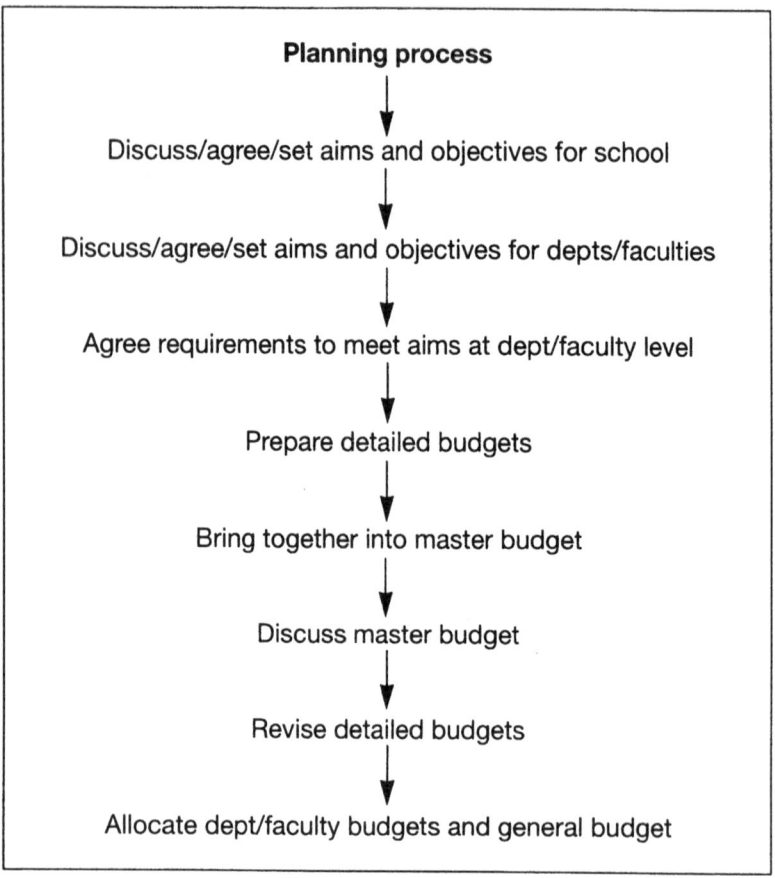

Planning process

Discuss/agree/set aims and objectives for school

Discuss/agree/set aims and objectives for depts/faculties

Agree requirements to meet aims at dept/faculty level

Prepare detailed budgets

Bring together into master budget

Discuss master budget

Revise detailed budgets

Allocate dept/faculty budgets and general budget

CHAPTER 4

Recording Financial Information

Legal requirements

There are certain legal requirements for accounting and financial information with which schools and LEAs are obliged to comply. These are:

1. Each LEA is required to complete an annual financial statement of the general schools' budget for schools covered by the LMS scheme, in accordance with the provisions of Section 42 of the Education Reform Act. This enables schools to check the accuracy of their budget share.
2. The school governors hold the budget and have to approve and forward a budget statement to the LEA for its approval.
3. The LEA overall budget has to be approved by the Secretary of State.
4. All schools are fully audited by LEA internal auditors every two or three years. Checks are carried out to ensure that monitoring systems are being used correctly.

Not only is it a legal requirement that proper records are kept of the financial dealings in the school, it is an important management tool. In this chapter we will consider the three main types of financial records:

- accounts
- a balance sheet
- spreadsheets.

We will also look at banking and petty cash.

The purpose of accounting

'Annual income twenty pounds, annual expenditure nineteen pounds nineteen shillings and sixpence, result happiness.
Annual income twenty pounds, annual expenditure twenty pounds ought and sixpence, result misery.'

Mr Micawber in Charles Dickens' David Copperfield

The problem Mr Micawber was facing, over a hundred years ago, is likely to be familiar to us today – the management of personal finance. Most of us are concerned to manage our affairs so that our normal expenditure is covered by our wages or salary. In other words, over a period of time – be it a week, a month or a year – we would like to generate a surplus of income over expenditure, ie make a profit.

Unfortunately life is made more complicated by the fact that, as well as income and expenditure, we may have some *assets* – possessions of value, or some other form of *wealth*.

The different forms of wealth can best be demonstrated using the following simple illustration of personal wealth.

Two individuals, Dave and Joe, work together and have identical wages or income. They also have a similar spending pattern. The one major difference is that Dave rents a council flat, whereas Joe is buying a house. Their respective income and expenditure each month is as follows:

Monthly transactions		Dave £	Joe £
Income:	Take home pay	1,500	1,500
Expenditure:	Property costs (including rates, services etc)	(750)	(1,000)
	Other expenditure (food, clothes, car etc)	(550)	(500)
	Monthly surplus	200	–

As things stand in the average year Dave generates a surplus of 12 x £200 = £2,400, which he puts into his building society account. Joe, on the other hand, saves nothing. Using this data, who do you think is better off?

It looks as though Dave is wealthier, using monthly surplus as a yardstick, but let us look a little closer. If we inspect their relative cash positions as they exist at the moment we discover the following:

Current cash positions	Dave £	Joe £
Accumulated savings	7,000	–

Although they are lodged in the building society Dave's savings can be classified as cash as they are easily convertible.

So who is better off on a cash basis?

Dave again appears to be in the best position, based on cash as a measure. Finally let us judge them by the assets they own (ignoring the contents of their properties which are roughly comparable, eg TVs, furniture etc).

Assets owned at the present time:	Dave £	Joe £
Second-hand car	4,000	4,000
Cash (in building society)	7,000	–
Property value	–	80,000
Less: Amount owing on mortgage	–	(60,000)
	11,000	24,000

Now which one do we consider better off? Who is the wealthier? This time Joe should have got your vote.

From our example we can see that there are several different ways of measuring finance. Dave, for example, has a greater annual surplus than Joe, and much better cash resources. Joe on the other hand could be called the wealthier because, given time, he could realize much greater value than Dave.

Although the simple financial records created in the illustration referred to individuals, the same principles apply to any business.

In business the three most important documents produced as financial reports, or summaries of accounts, are:

1. The *surplus* (or deficit) calculated by subtracting expenditure from earnings over a given time period. This is otherwise known as the profit (or loss) generated during the period.
2. A *statement* on the cash position (otherwise know as the liquidity position).
3. The *wealth* or *value of assets* of the organization/individual at a point in time. Also included in this statement are any amounts owing to and any amounts owed by others.

This applies whether it be for individuals, partnerships, companies or international corporations. So, although a business may have many times more transactions than an individual, the accounts will be put together using the same principles.

Furthermore the simple surplus, cash and wealth statements developed above are an essential part of an accounting system.

What can we conclude from the way the simple accounts were drawn up for Dave and Joe?

1. In order to produce the figures used, *records* had to be kept of all the transactions occurring.
2. The transactions were summarized to give *financial reports*. These demonstrated either the results over a period of time (eg the savings in a year), or the situation at a given point in time (eg the value of the house at a particular time).

A definition of the purpose of accounting might therefore be: 'To provide records of all financial transactions, so that the financial position of an organization can be determined. To produce reports showing this financial position to the owners or managers of the organization and any other interested parties.'

By 'financial position' we mean:

- the surplus or profit generated;
- the cash position;
- a statement of wealth at a particular time:
  - the assets of the organization;
  - any amounts owed to others (our creditors);
  - any amounts owed to the organization by others (our debtors).

This purpose of accounting is as true for a school as it is for a business. To keep informed of your financial position you need to keep accurate records. These will be the basis of day-to-day financial management and future decisions.

How do accounting records operate?

In our definition of the purpose of accounting we stated that a key element was the recording and reporting of financial transactions. We now need to examine how the recording is done.

The basic transaction recording process or *book-keeping method* we use today has been developed over the centuries. It is most easily explained by following its development over time – both public and private book-keeping occurred in ancient Egyptian, Greek and Roman times.

In the public sector the development of community organizations in ancient civilizations was accompanied by the need for appointed officials to account for their use of public funds. In other words they were obliged to keep records of, and account for, income and expenditure, and have their records checked (or audited) by other officials.

In the private sector, on the other hand, merchants and landowners would ask their agents to present an account of activities relating to the business or property. It became the custom for the owners to hire professional examiners of accounts – auditors – to check the accounts. These accounts were often presented verbally and the name auditor comes from the Latin *audire*, to hear.

These original accounts were merely a list of income and expenditure, the sort of simple accounts that are still used for small organizations such as sports clubs today. However, by the fifteenth century, the larger Italian merchants had outgrown this system. Much of their wealth was tied up in stocks of merchandise, so they needed a system that could cope with valuations of assets and wealth. A system was therefore developed that could not only deal with different types of business transactions, but was also self-checking – the *double-entry system*. This system, first described by Pacioli in 1494, forms the basis for book-keeping and accounts as we know them today.

Since the fifteenth century the major change in business has been the increasing complexity of ownership – from single merchants through joint ventures to today's multinationals with many thousands of shareholders. The double-entry system has been robust enough to cope with these changes despite the demands for greater accountability as owners have become more remote from day-to-day commercial operations.

Schools may not have the complexity of ownership that large corporations have, but their funding comes from a variety of sources (LEA, government and generated income) and they have a number of interested parties to whom they must demonstrate their efficiency (LEA, governors and parents).

Double-entry book-keeping

So what distinguishes double-entry book-keeping from other systems? Well, as the name suggests, each transaction is recorded twice – as a *debit* and as a *credit*. You may be familiar with these terms – a debit being money spent or owed to us, and a credit being income, or money owed by us to others.

The advantage of each entry being made twice is that, at the end of the time period, the value of credits should equal the total of debits. This is a basic test that the arithmetic is accurate. The statement of total debits and credits is known as a *trial balance*. The way in which entries appear in a trial balance is shown below.

Item	Debit (DR)	Credit (CR)
Fixed assets	X	
Creditors (amounts owing)		X
Revenue from sales		X
Expenditure	X	
Cash	X	

Before leaving this topic, let us see how each transaction is entered twice in basic books, by using as an example a few transactions that might take place in a school. In companies, the basic books of account are divided into *ledgers*, eg sales ledger, purchase ledger, general ledger, cash book etc. The name derives from the days when separate books were kept for each type of transaction. Nowadays, the entries are more likely to be input in to a computer; however, the ledger structure will still be maintained within the computerized system. In schools it is unlikely that separate ledgers will be kept although it may be useful for larger schools.

Example of double-entry book keeping		
	Debit	**Credit**
LEA Grant		200,000
debit cash book, cash invested	200,000	
Maintenance charge	4,000	
cash book payment		4,000
Materials charged to account	3,000	
cash book payment		3,000
Wages charged to account	160,000	
cash book payment		160,000
Income from lettings		1,500
cash book receipt	1,500	

At this stage we merely wish to demonstrate that each transaction is matched by an equal and opposite entry, and that therefore total debits equal total credits. It is important to remember that underpinning each line of the report there may be many individual double-entry records.

ACTIVITY 1

We saw in the text that a debit is money owing to us, an expense incurred, or an asset owned, whilst a credit is money we owe, income or capital invested.

Mark the following transactions as debit (DR) or credits (CR) – ignore the equal and opposite entry.

(a) An electricity bill due for payment

(b) An invoice outstanding for sales made

(c) A bank overdraft

(d) Components purchased

(e) A factory purchased

(f) VAT owed to HM Customs and Excise

(g) Cash sales made

The answers to this exercise are given after the Summary at the end of this chapter. Descriptions of the terms are also given in the Glossary at the end of the book.

Spreadsheets and balance sheets

Companies need to keep detailed records of all their transactions and produce a full set of accounts annually for tax purposes. Schools may not need to carry out exactly the same procedure, but it is essential that governors and the senior management team are aware of exactly what records they are required to keep for their LEA.

Whatever the exact requirements, two useful devices are spreadsheets and balance sheets and anyone who has to produce financial information should know the purpose and basic mechanics of these.

Spreadsheets

As the name implies these show a 'spread' of all the financial information in one document. All the transactions which take place are shown on the spreadsheet. As much detail can be added as is needed.

As information is added and changed (eg new income added on, expenditure taken off) the balance of money in the organization will change.

A spreadsheet is a dynamic working document and should reflect the day-to-day changes in the financial situation as transactions take place. In businesses, spreadsheets may be updated daily or even hourly. For schools this is unlikely to be necessary as most transactions take place over longer time-scales. It is up to the individual user to determine how often this updating needs to take place, but this may be governed by the frequency of financial reports required by the LEA. It is never a good idea to leave it too long as it may then entail a lot of work or the risk of forgetting some data.

Nowadays most organizations use computers for keeping their spreadsheets up to date. We will come back to this in the section on computers later in this chapter.

The balance sheet

A balance sheet is a picture of an organization taken at a particular moment – a kind of financial freeze-frame: 'a statement of the financial position (that is, assets, liabilities and capital) of an organization at a particular point in time'. Moreover it is a measurement of the wealth of the organization at that moment. In companies it could be compared with an earlier balance sheet, and so used to assess the growth of the company in the intervening period.

Why is it called a balance sheet? Because the assets, liabilities and capital of the organization will all *balance* at any one time. In other words the sources and potential sources of investment balance the uses and potential uses of funds, ie the total of debits must balance the total of credits. Now we'll look at a typical balance sheet.

Financial skills for teachers

Fund: School Budget Share	Allocation	Est to Date	Commitment	Expenditure	Variance
Heading: Employees					
Bud/Acc: Teaching Staff	500000.00	92338.00	429598.96	132603.34	40265.34
Bud/Acc: Ancillary Staff	100084.49	0.00	93738.69	31041.86	31041.86
Bud/Acc: LEA Supply Staff (Sickness)	10062.64	0.00	0.00	377.45	377.45
Bud/Acc: Hourly Paid Staff	20000.00	3736.00	13913.03	4159.48	423.48
Bud/Acc: Other Employee Expenses	300.00	0.00	280.77	19.23	19.23
Bud/Acc: Agency Staff	25272.00	0.00	0.00	14550.00	14550.00
Bud/Acc: Clerks to Governing Bodies	482.04	0.00	363.00	119.04	119.04
Subtotals	656201.17	96074.00	537894.45	182870.40	86796.40
Heading: Capitation					
Bud/Acc: Capitation	57603.90	0.00	5978.20	5889.59	5889.59
Subtotals	57603.90	0.00	5978.20	5889.59	5889.59
Heading: Premises Related Costs					
Bud/Acc: Electricity	7000.00	1223.00	5740.00	1430.70	207.70
Bud/Acc: Gas	7000.00	1223.00	5997.27	1362.04	139.04
Bud/Acc: Water and Sewage Metered	2300.00	667.00	1633.00	976.14	309.14
Bud/Acc: Rents/UBR/Water Rates	13069.00	0.00	0.00	0.00	0.00
Bud/Acc: Grounds Maintenance	855.00	0.00	0.00	854.81	854.81
Bud/Acc: Security/Alarms	250.00	0.00	0.00	98.00	98.00
Bud/Acc: Furniture	0.00	0.00	0.00	0.00	0.00
Bud/Acc: Cleaning Materials	676.41	0.00	538.41	138.00	138.00
Bud/Acc: General Repairs and Maintenance	11126.82	0.00	3826.16	850.50	850.50
Bud/Acc: Refuse Collection	1020.00	0.00	0.00	0.00	0.00
Bud/Acc: Contract Cleaning	19300.00	4610.00	3216.00	5379.41	769.41
Bud/Acc: Fire Extinguishers	200.00	0.00	0.00	0.00	0.00
Subtotals	62797.23	7723.00	20950.84	11089.60	3366.60
Heading: Income					
Bud/Acc: Sale of Goods	0.00	0.00	0.00	0.00	0.00
Bud/Acc: Miscellaneous income	−2302.34	0.00	0.00	−2302.34	2302.34−
Bud/Acc: Liabilities Credit from 94/95	−10709.65	0.00	0.00	−10709.65	10709.65−
Bud/Acc: School Meals Recharge	0.00	0.00	0.00	0.00	0.00
Bud/Acc: School Fund/PTA donations	0.00	0.00	0.00	0.00	0.00
Bud/Acc: Exam Fees income	0.00	0.00	0.00	0.00	0.00
Bud/Acc: Telephone call income	−25.53	0.00	0.00	−25.53	25.53−
Bud/Acc: Lettings	0.00	0.00	0.00	0.00	0.00
Subtotals	−13037.52	0.00	0.00	−13037.52	13037.52−

Fund: School Budget Share	Allocation	Est to Date	Commitment	Expenditure	Variance
Heading: Supplies and services					
Bud/Acc: Telephones	1350.00	372.00	978.00	333.01	38.99-
Bud/Acc: Annual Maintenance Contracts	3720.00	0.00	638.90	886.91	886.91
Bud/Acc: Postage	550.00	100.00	0.00	112.75	12.75
Bud/Acc: Transport/Travel	1900.00	0.00	0.00	534.00	534.00
Bud/Acc: External Exams/Linked Courses	0.00	0.00	0.00	0.00	0.00
Bud/Acc: Swimming	1850.00	0.00	0.00	540.00	540.00
Bud/Acc: Governing Body Expenses	115.00	0.00	0.00	0.00	0.00
Bud/Acc: Insurances	500.00	0.00	0.00	0.00	0.00
Subtotals	9985.00	472.00	1616.90	2406.67	1934.67
Heading: In Service Training (non GEST)					
Bud/Acc: Cover for Training	830.00	0.00	0.00	0.00	0.00
Bud/Acc: Materials	0.00	0.00	0.00	0.00	0.00
Bud/Acc: Course Fees	375.00	0.00	0.00	0.00	0.00
Bud/Acc: Miscellaneous Expenses	300.00	0.00	300.00	0.00	0.00
Subtotals	1505.00	0.00	300.00	0.00	0.00
Heading: Professional Fees					
Bud/Acc: Schools Financial Services	0.00	0.00	0.00	0.00	0.00
Bud/Acc: Peripatetic Music Tuition	7765.00	0.00	4447.50	0.00	0.00
Subtotals	7765.00	0.00	4447.50	0.00	0.00
Heading: Orders/Invoices from 94/95					
Bud/Acc: SBS Orders/Invoices from 94/95	5100.00	0.00	5045.00	220.58	220.58
Bud/Acc: GEST Liabilities from 94/95	428.00	0.00	111.00	0.00	0.00
Subtotals	5528.00	0.00	5156.00	220.58	220.58
Fund Reserves (unallocated)	148073.22				
FUND TOTALS	936421.00	104269.00	576343.89	189439.32	85170.32

Account Summary for Financial Year 95/96 in a Greater London School

Notes. *Allocation* is the amount allocated to that heading (eg 'Teaching staff') from the delegated budget set in April. *Est to date* is what the school believes it has already spent (calculated from the LEA computer print out). *Commitment* is what the school is already committed to spend for the rest of that financial year. *Expenditure* is what has actually been spent to date (ie April, May and June in the example shown). *Variance* is the difference between the estimated expenditure to date and the actual spend to date. (NB Where the variance is shown as negative it is an *Under*spend. This is different to normal business accounting conventions where *Over*spend is normally shown as negative.)

ACTIVITY 2

Using the information contained in the balance sheet (pages 42–43) answer the following questions.

1. Is the expenditure on teaching staff under or over budget?

2. Which has cost the school more to date – electricity or gas?

3. Has the school earned any income from lettings this year?

4. Has any money been spent on peripatetic music teaching so far this year?

5. How much has been put into the reserve this year?

The answers to these questions are given after the Summary at the end of this chapter.

In an annual report the current period balance sheet should always be accompanied by the previous period's balance sheet. In this way a comparison between the two statements can be made and the movements during the intervening period reviewed.

Computer systems

The great value of computers is that they can process vast amounts of information very quickly. Once a program is set up, by changing one figure we can see the knock-on effect for the whole financial system. The 'down' side of computers, though, is that they can only process the information they are given. If the user inputs inaccurate data, the computer program will give back inaccurate data. Accuracy in both setting up and using the system is essential.

Security

There are guidelines on using computer systems for financial information given in the Ofsted document *Keeping Your Balance*. In essence this states that it is important that financial information held on computer is properly protected and backed-up and that access is restricted only to authorized users. Further, the use of computer systems in schools, particularly for administrative purposes, requires the registration of governing bodies and headteachers under the Data Protection Act 1984. The Act imposes requirements of openness and good practice on computer users. It sets up a public register of users who hold personal data and requires them to comply with the code of practice incorporated in the Act, known as the Data Protection Principles. LEA-maintained schools should determine whether they need to register independently or are covered under their LEA's data protection registration.

Back-up procedures should be set by the head and rigorously maintained for security in case the data is wiped out or the computer stolen. A suggested system is that on a *daily* or *weekly basis* (depending how often data is changed):

Copy all financial files on to disk or tape; store disks or tapes in locked fireproof cabinet away from the computer (eg off site).

The school should also take advice in making a 'disaster recovery plan' in the event of losing all its data.

Only authorized staff should have access to the hardware and software used for school management. In addition to physical access this should include the use of passwords (at least two 'tiers') which are changed regularly.

Viruses

All disks put into management machines should be virus checked before being used. A separate computer for this is probably a luxury few schools could afford, but virus checking should be carried out on a computer where loss of data would not be disastrous and one which is not linked to others on a network. It is essential that only authorized and virus-checked software is used on computers which carry important management data.

Reporting using the computer

Each LEA has its own reporting procedure relating to its computerized financial systems. The purpose of this is to share information between the LEA and school regularly in a structured way and to ensure that accurate records are being kept. The table below is an example of the monitoring procedure in one LEA.

Month:	Period:	
COMPUTER SYSTEM 'A' PERIOD END: Date as per message on Main Menu		
TICK	**ACTION REQUIRED**	**ROUTE**
☐	1 FREEZE PERIOD	PERIOD END – FREEZE ACCOUNTS – FREEZE
☐	2 EXPORT TO SYSTEM 'F' (Produce Output Journals)	PERIOD END – EXPORT DATA – 'F' EXPORT
☐	3 PRODUCE CITD REPORTS	PERIOD END – PERIOD END REPORTS – CITDS REPORTS
☐	4 ARCHIVE	ACCOUNTS – ARCHIVE – RUN ARCHIVING
☐	5 PRINT AUDIT TRAIL (You will need wide bed paper)	ACCOUNTS – ACCOUNTS REPORTS – AUDIT TRAIL
☐	6 SAVE AUDIT TRAIL TO DISK (You will need one HD disk for 1995/96)	ACCOUNTS – AUDIT TRAIL TO DISKETTE
'F' PERIOD END: RECEIPT OF 'F' TAB AND DOWNLOAD DISK		
TICK	**ACTION REQUIRED**	**ROUTE**
☐	1 CHECK 'F' PAYROLL CHARGES (Raising tab queries as appropriate)	
☐	2 CHECK OUTPUT JOURNAL AGAINST 'F' TAB	
☐	3 LOAD DOWNLOAD DISK (Follow on screen instructions)	PERIOD END – IMPORT DATA – PAYROLL DATA
☐	4 PRINT 'F' RECONCILIATION REPORT (Investigate non-zero variance)	PERIOD END – PERIOD END REPORTS – 'F' RECONCILIATION REPORT

☐	5	PRINT ALL ACCOUNTS RECONCILIATION	ACCOUNTS – ACCOUNTS REPORTS – ALL ACCOUNTS RECONCILIATION

PRODUCE A MONITORING STATEMENT

TICK	ACTION REQUIRED	ROUTE
☐ 1	ACCESS SYSTEM 'S'	MONITORING – CREATE – 5 DIGIT LEVEL – PERIOD N0 (You can say 'no' to question about comments)
☐ 2	PRINT MONITORING	MONITORING – PRINT – PERIOD No.
☐ 3	ADD COMMENTS	MONITORING – ADD/AMEND COMMENTS NB If you have amended profile to adjust monitoring statement you will need to CREATE monitoring statement again.
☐ 4	RESERVES ANALYSIS	RESERVES – REPORTS – AUTHORISED PLAN

RETURNS REQUIRED FOR CENTRE: GIVE OR SEND TO SCHOOL FINANCE OFFICER

TICK	PLEASE ENSURE THAT THE SCHOOL NAME APPEARS ON ALL REPORTS
☐ 1	MONTHLY MONITORING STATEMENT AT 5 DIGIT LEVEL, WITH COMMENTS
☐ 2	'F' RECONCILIATION REPORT ON WHICH EXPLANATION FOR VARIANCES ARE NOTED AND TAB QUERIES ARE ATTACHED.
☐ 3	ALL ACCOUNTS RECONCILIATION REPORT.

Notes. *System 'A'* is the LEA Accounting System. *System 'F'* is the LEA Finance Information System.

Banking arrangements

The proper administration of bank accounts is a fundamental financial control. In particular, regular bank reconciliations are essential. Reconciliations prove that balances are correct and provide assurance that the underlying accounts have been properly compiled and are accurate. Again, detailed standards for banking arrangements are given in Ofsted's *Keeping Your Balance*.

The Secretary of State has determined that all secondary schools with full delegation should have the opportunity to pay for all non-employee expenditure from their own bank accounts. The principles for the operation of the scheme were laid down as follows:

1. The school can choose its own bank (from an approved list supplied by the LEA).
2. The account will be used to pay all non-employee costs.
3. The account may attract and the school may retain interest.
4. Funds must be credited to the account on a regular basis.
5. Any charges made by the LEA must be clearly specified and justified, eg recovery of loss of interest on central bank balances.
6. Loans and arranged overdrafts are not allowed.

Basically there are three options for schools:

1. to retain the existing arrangements for the payment of accounts established by the LEA;
2. to take up a cheque book account under a favourable group scheme negotiated by the LEA with their own bank;
3. to take up a cheque book account with some other approved financial institution.

There are obviously advantages to schools in having their own bank account. These include:

- earning interest on the account;
- access to the full range of banking facilities;
- ability to settle accounts quickly and therefore negotiate discounts with suppliers.

It is essential to negotiate low or nil charges on some types of account.

However, there are also disadvantages:

- security for cheque books;

- producing VAT returns for the LEA;
- payment to the LEA for loss of interest;
- need for regular audit and financial procedures.

It is up to the governors and headteacher to decide what is in the best interests of the school.

Petty cash

Petty cash is administratively convenient for making small payments, particularly if the signatories of the main bank account are not available. However, cash is vulnerable and must be properly controlled. The governing body will need to ensure that the amount of cash holding is appropriate, that it is used for approved purposes, that proper records are maintained and that there are regular reconciliations and occasional spot checks to verify that the sums in hand are correct.

Large sums of cash should not be kept on the school premises, neither should they be taken off the school premises without proper procedure and authority.

Each school employee authorized to hold petty cash should be responsible for:

- obtaining proper vouchers and receipts for all cash payments made;
- obtaining a receipt or acknowledgement of payment which identifies any VAT paid;
- ensuring the safe custody of cash;
- producing on demand to the headteacher, auditor or other authorized person cash or vouchers to the total of the amount drawn;
- submitting regular claims for reimbursement, properly certified and supported by vouchers and receipts.

Summary

There are regulations and legal obligations for keeping accounting records which must be observed. In addition, keeping good accounts is essential to the good management of every organization.

Accounts are records of financial transactions which have taken place. They include different formats for different purposes.

Double-entry book-keeping allows us to make sure that credits and debits are balanced.

Spreadsheets allow us to track financial activity and see the state of our finances on an ongoing basis. A balance sheet is a snapshot of the income and expenditure, assets, liabilities and capital of the organization at a given time.

Computerized accounts save time but information must be input accurately for them to be useful.

Arrangements for banking can be made by each school in the light of the advantages and disadvantages compared with its own needs.

Security of all financial recording and associated items (eg cheque books) is essential.

Answers to Activity 1

(a) (CR) – money owed by us.

(b) (DR) – money owed to us.

(c) (CR) – money owed by us.

(d) (DR) – expenditure made.

(e) (DR) – expenditure made.

(f) (CR) – money owed by us.

(g) (CR) – income.

Answers to Activity 2

1. Actual expenditure of £132,603.34 plus the committed expenditure of £429,598.96 comes to £562,202.30. This is an overspend of £62,202.30 over the allocated budget. The estimate to date of £92,338 plus the commitment of £429,598.96 comes to £521,936.96. This is an overspend of £21,936.96 above the allocated budget.

Accounts are records of financial transactions which have taken place. They include different formats for different purposes.

Double-entry book-keeping allows us to make sure that credits and debits are balanced.

Spreadsheets allow us to track financial activity and see the state of our finances on an ongoing basis. A balance sheet is a snapshot of the income and expenditure, assets, liabilities and capital of the organization at a given time.

Computerized accounts save time but information must be input accurately for them to be useful.

Arrangements for banking can be made by each school in the light of the advantages and disadvantages compared with its own needs.

Security of all financial recording and associated items (eg cheque books) is essential.

Answers to Activity 1

(a) (CR) – money owed by us.

(b) (DR) – money owed to us.

(c) (CR) – money owed by us.

(d) (DR) – expenditure made.

(e) (DR) – expenditure made.

(f) (CR) – money owed by us.

(g) (CR) – income.

Answers to Activity 2

1. Actual expenditure of £132,603.34 plus the committed expenditure of £429,598.96 comes to £562,202.30. This is an overspend of £62,202.30 over the allocated budget. The estimate to date of £92,338 plus the commitment of £429,598.96 comes to £521,936.96. This is an overspend of £21,936.96 above the allocated budget.

- producing VAT returns for the LEA;
- payment to the LEA for loss of interest;
- need for regular audit and financial procedures.

It is up to the governors and headteacher to decide what is in the best interests of the school.

Petty cash

Petty cash is administratively convenient for making small payments, particularly if the signatories of the main bank account are not available. However, cash is vulnerable and must be properly controlled. The governing body will need to ensure that the amount of cash holding is appropriate, that it is used for approved purposes, that proper records are maintained and that there are regular reconciliations and occasional spot checks to verify that the sums in hand are correct.

Large sums of cash should not be kept on the school premises, neither should they be taken off the school premises without proper procedure and authority.

Each school employee authorized to hold petty cash should be responsible for:

- obtaining proper vouchers and receipts for all cash payments made;
- obtaining a receipt or acknowledgement of payment which identifies any VAT paid;
- ensuring the safe custody of cash;
- producing on demand to the headteacher, auditor or other authorized person cash or vouchers to the total of the amount drawn;
- submitting regular claims for reimbursement, properly certified and supported by vouchers and receipts.

Summary

There are regulations and legal obligations for keeping accounting records which must be observed. In addition, keeping good accounts is essential to the good management of every organization.

CHAPTER 5

Suppliers

Central purchasing v. local arrangements

In the past LEAs controlled all the purchasing for schools. This had the advantage that individual schools did not have the responsibility of finding suppliers, arranging payment and handling invoices. It had the disadvantage that they were limited to using the suppliers decided by the LEA, so sometimes could not buy exactly what they wanted. Although the LEA could usually negotiate good prices for bulk orders this was not always the best price available, because their slow payment meant that suppliers were sometimes unwilling to offer a really low price.

Now, in most instances, schools are able to deal directly with their own chosen suppliers, although in some cases LEAs still offer a central purchasing function for certain items, such as stationery, textiles, science equipment and filing cabinets. The advantages of schools dealing directly with their own supplies are:

- the ability to select exactly who they wish to deal with;
- the ability to negotiate their own delivery schedules, prices and payment terms.

The disadvantages are:

- time required to find suppliers;
- time required to negotiate deals;
- handling of payments.

Although seemingly onerous at first, most schools prefer the new arrangements. The time invested in your relationships with suppliers can pay good dividends in the end. It may be a long-term investment, but is usually worthwhile, and we will talk more about this later in this chapter.

Finding and checking out suppliers

Finding a new supplier for the first time can be a daunting task. Take the example of a teacher new to a school and new to the area wanting to buy some science equipment or a computer for the department. There are so many suppliers offering deals on this and that, it is difficult to know where to begin. Particular types of materials and equipment have specific needs, and books need a different approach, but you must always prepare yourself before you approach any supplier. There are certain key questions which should be asked *whatever* you are buying.

Before you start thinking about a supplier

- What is the purpose of what you are buying? (Have a detailed account of age range, proposed use, learning needs, required lifespan, use, environment etc.)
- Does what you need have to fit in with an existing series of books or other piece of equipment?
- Do you have a delivery date requirement?
- Do you have a price range in mind? (If you have no idea, ask colleagues and look at catalogues so you have a starting point for negotiation.)
- Does the LEA have a preferred supplier or have they banned the use of any supplier?

On deciding which suppliers to approach

Before you begin

Does the school have a preferred supplier for this type of purchase? Do any of your colleagues have advice on a suitable supplier?

When you start talking to suppliers

Checklist of general questions

- Do you need a specific brand? If so, which suppliers stock it?
- Of those that stock it, what is their location?
- Do they charge for delivery?
- Do you have particular delivery date requirement? If so, can they meet it?
- What are their payment terms?
- Do they give discount to schools?
- Will they negotiate on price? Is the price affected by payment?
- *NB Does their price include or exclude VAT?*

Checklist of technical items

- Do they provide training in the product if required? If so, at what cost?
- Do they provide on-site maintenance? At what cost? How quickly?
- What other 'add-ons' can they supply?
- Can you upgrade later?
- What other support do they offer?

You need to consider all these points at the outset because it can save time and trouble in the future. Cost is not always the best factor on which to judge a supplier. For example with equipment like a computer you may require on-site maintenance because the supplier is a long distance away. If they cannot offer this type of support it may be worth considering an alternative supplier who is nearer although the initial cost is higher.

Technical equipment requires more specialist knowledge of the product and how you will use it. It may be sensible to seek specialist help from a colleague or someone in the LEA (computers are a particular case in point and some LEAs have specialist departments to offer such advice). When buying any piece of equipment that has to work with another, such as a printer attached to a computer, it is essential that they will work together. Therefore it is sometimes better to buy both from the same supplier, even if the cost is slightly more. This way, if one piece goes wrong, the supplier cannot easily blame the other piece of kit!

In most cases companies which are offering to supply goods or a service are genuine – the dishonest ones are the minority. However, you have to be aware of the possibility and take reasonable steps to avoid the school losing out. More likely, though, will be those who offer something which is not intentionally dishonest or substandard but may not be what you require or may not be up to the job you need it to do. For example a piece of equipment which is perfectly adequate for home use may not be robust enough to withstand the use it will get in a school day in and day out. For this reason it is probably best to deal with suppliers who are used to doing business with schools or similar establishments.

This does not mean that you should never try someone new – all suppliers started somewhere and giving a smaller company your business may result in excellent service. Service is an important factor. A supplier who gives good service is worth much in terms of the time and trouble they can save you. If you want advice or help it could cost a lot of money in wasted time if you have to keep chasing them on the phone, they don't return calls or they are unsympathetic to your needs. A supplier who turns out to be unreliable and does not deliver on time can cause you a great deal of trouble, especially if you need something in a hurry.

So how can you tell a good supplier from a poor one? It may not be easy – and experience is the best teacher. The following guidelines may be helpful:

Choosing for quality

Word of mouth

Recommendation by an experienced colleague whom you trust is probably the best way to start.

Other customers

If you do not already know someone who has used a particular supplier but this supplier matches all your needs – ask the supplier if you can talk to other customers.

A test

Are they prepared to let you try something out? A test or demonstration where you can try hands on – especially over a period of time – is very useful.

Start small

If possible start off with a fairly small transaction with a new supplier – preferably something which is not crucial to your work. If that works well and the supplier gives good service, try them for something bigger or more important next time.

Be fair

Don't be unreasonable in your demands, explain exactly what you need and why and give the supplier any parameters (eg delivery dates). Expecting them to read your mind, then blaming them when they fail to do so, is not helpful.

Supplier development

As you get to know your pupils you build up a relationship with them. They will understand how you work, what you require of them and how to make the most of your experience. You will get to know how they learn best and what motivates them. In this way both sides benefit. Similarly building up a long-term relationship in any business dealings you have is better than a brief encounter. If you spend time getting to know your suppliers and what their needs are you will be in a better position to make the best use of their services.

It may sound a bit extravagant, spending time finding out how your suppliers work and what their needs are, but it is an investment worth making. Take the example of buying artwork and printed materials.

Case study

In June the head of English was asked to organize the production of a brochure about the school. She asked her colleagues for information on each of their departments, then wrote the text. She checked it for accuracy with the other departments and circulated it among the governors and senior management team for approval. This took five weeks in total.

It then needed a layout and printing. She went directly to a printer who had worked successfully for another local school and asked him if he could print the brochure. He asked how many pages and what colours. She told him four pages of A4, single colour times 500 copies, and got a quote. He gave her a price and delivery date three weeks hence. It seemed expensive so she asked for a quote from another printer for whom she had seen an advertisement. The price was better, so she got an order raised and a week later went to see the second printer, assuming he could meet the same delivery date of three weeks. This gave her a delivery date of mid-August – in plenty of time for the selection by the next year's intake in the autumn term.

But when she got to the printer he had been expecting finished artwork, not just typed sheets, and he could not organize the artwork. She then asked the head of Art for advice. He recommended that they give the layout to the year 10 art pupils to do on their computer as an exercise; but they could not start until the new term. This seemed like a good solution and would save money. The exercise started in early September, and took another three weeks. Then she rang the printer, but by this time he was busy and could not start the job for two weeks. So she contacted the first printer. He could do the job and was prepared to try to finish in two weeks, subject to sight of the artwork. The problem was that when he looked at the design it required six pages, not the original four, and would have to be made into a fold out leaflet (expensive due to the larger paper required) or it would have to be made into an eight page booklet. In addition, his computer system was not compatible with the school's so there was extra cost in bureau fees to get the work transferred.

The end result was a more expensive job which arrived almost too late for distribution to prospective parents for the next year.

Had the teacher concerned visited the two printers at the outset they would probably have helped by advising her on what needed to be done and then she could have:

- found out all the processes required and so delivered what the printer needed;
- briefed the pupils to design within certain limits;
- written her text to suit the design and required size;
- saved time by starting the design work while researching the text.

Supplier development is a two-way process – it is important to find out how your suppliers work. You will then learn what they need from you to help them do their best. At the same time they can learn more about you – understand your needs, find out why you have to carry out certain procedures or need equipment to a very specific standard to meet curriculum or examination requirements.

That way you will learn to give them:

- the time they need to do the job properly;
- the detailed specification in language they understand so they get the order right;
- the correct 'raw materials' (as in the case of the printing example) so they don't waste time.

They will learn:

- why you need things when you do;
- why you need certain specifications and when a substitute will or will not do;
- when and how you pay.

Any company worth dealing with will understand the value of a relationship where you talk to each other, and any company with common sense will know that it is far better to keep existing customers than lose them and have to look for new ones all the time. This mutual understanding will, over a period, build up a trusting relationship where you will be able to help and support each other, so achieving a much better service with less hassle.

ACTIVITY

Make a list of all the suppliers used directly by your department. Next to each name on the list note:

    Do I fully understand what they do?
    Have I a personal contact I can ask for advice?

If the answer to either of these questions is 'No', then make an ACTION PLAN of what you can do to remedy this. Ideas could include a visit to them, they visit you, or you could ask advice from a colleague who has worked with them before. The table below shows how you could lay this out.

ITEM	SUPPLIER	WHAT THEY DO	WHAT WE DO	ACTION
Ex. Books	Central purchasing			None
Printing	J J Press	No	No	Visit them 2:10
Computers	C C Computers	Yes	No	Visit us 12:11

Internal customer/supplier relationships

In a school there are people with experience and expertise in many areas, some of whom will have worked in commercial organizations outside education. This is a source of advice and support which all the staff can tap into. I do not mean the expectation that the Home Economics department will always provide the food for school functions (unless it is on a business basis!). Going back to our example of the school brochure – had the head of English asked the head of Art for advice at an early stage, he might have helped her to avoid some of the pitfalls.

The pupils and parents are not the only customers for the school. Within the school there is the possibility of staff being customers of some departments, and suppliers to others. For example, if the Geography department needs the pupils to draw weather graphs, who should teach them? Perhaps an agreement between the geographers and mathematicians could save duplication of effort or, worse, the confusion of the pupils through being shown too many different techniques. Team teaching and sharing of ideas is now widely accepted, but the relationship of seeing each other as customers or suppliers may help to support that.

Customers need: *a service that satisfies their needs*.
Suppliers can: *give a service to help and support the successful fulfillment of the customers' needs*.

Ultimately the pupils and their parents are the customers, but they are only the last part in a chain which involves all the school.

Summary

Purchasing via the LEA has advantages in time and convenience, and may be cheaper; but purchasing directly may provide a better service with lower costs. Whichever method is used it should be carefully monitored to make sure that the school is getting the best service and value for money.

Suppliers can assist purchasers with advice. It is helpful if you understand what they do and how they do it to get the best from their products or services.

Developing a good relationship with suppliers is a long-term investment worth making. Customer/supplier relationships can also exist within your school and this can bring benefits through sharing information and advice as well as by undertaking tasks to help each other.

CHAPTER 6

Purchasing and Payment

Purchasing

One of the aims of LMS is to give schools with financial delegation freedom over purchasing arrangements. At the same time schools must maintain proper accountability for and control over the spending of public money. They will also want to obtain the best value for money from their purchases. As we said in the last chapter, this does not necessarily mean the lowest price, but the most cost effective. That is the correct quality, quantity, delivery time and service for the best price. Making sure you are being offered a reasonable price is important, and you can do this by:

- consulting your LEA supplies department;
- checking trade journals and catalogues;
- seeking quotations and tenders.

Many LEAs will have central supplies or purchasing organizations which will have negotiated contracts for the majority of materials commonly used by schools. Other items, such as fuel, may be purchased by the local authority on behalf of schools. Economies of scale can mean that competitive terms are available. Schools are not obliged to use these services, but good prices and the availability of expert help from the central function means that it is certainly worth considering.

It is the responsibility of the governing body to ensure that the school obtains the best value for money in its purchases. It can do this by testing the market before the school is committed to any expenditure. However in reality small purchases by individual departments may not go through such a procedure, so it is sensible that anyone involved in any purchase on behalf of the school is aware of the basic requirements and methods. Normally the governing body will specify a sum above which all quotations should be viewed by the governors, also that purchases above another agreed sum should be put to tender (see 'Terminology' below). Guidelines on the amounts and regulations for tenders or competitive quotes are normally laid down by the LEA. One example, from the City of Birmingham Standing Orders relating to contracts, states: 'No contract between £2,500 and £20,000 inclusive in value or amount for the supply of goods, materials or services or the execution of any work shall be entered into unless not less than three written quotations have been obtained.'

The governors and senior management team of the school should make sure that they know what the regulations are in their own LEA and take steps to comply. There are usually, also, rules about how such quotations are to be presented, when and how they are to be opened and guidelines on making the decisions. Again the school and governors must know what these are and take steps to ensure that they are complied with.

Purchase, lease or rent

Certain items of equipment such as photocopiers and telephone networks may require decisions on whether purchase, lease or rent would be the best option. Each has advantages and the school should weigh up the pros and cons carefully.

Purchasing will tie the buyer to that piece of equipment for some time. The equipment may become out of date before it has earned its cost.

Leasing enables a school to update the equipment at the end of the lease. Leasing may include some form of maintenance – the school should enquire about this and whether or not extra cost is involved. Lease – purchase contracts may be available, which mean that the school will become the owner when the lease expires. This may or may not be wanted, so the relevant costs and advantages need to be considered. Make sure you are not committing the school or yourself to ongoing expenditure that could become a burden for several years.

Rentals are usually high, but should include maintenance and updating clauses in the contract. With certain types of equipment this is advantageous.

It is advisable when a major acquisition is being considered that all these options are explored. Again the LEA or legal adviser should be consulted as the school will need to examine not only the cost effectiveness of one method or another but also the terms of the contract. Once a lease or rental has been agreed the school will be bound by the terms of the contract until it expires.

Terminology

When dealing with financial matters it is important that you understand the difference between certain terms, as they can form part of a legal contract. The terms 'estimate' and 'quote' are sometimes wrongly used as meaning similar things. They do not mean the same, and the difference is an important one.

Estimates

When you are going to make a purchase or have a job done you will want to know what it will cost. Sometimes it is easy to put an exact price on something – particularly if you are buying a specific item such as a book or a piece of furniture. Sometimes it is less easy – this is especially true when you are having maintenance work carried out or buying a service.

Case study

A painter was asked to give a price for repainting the classrooms in one building of a school. He visited the school and looked at the classrooms. He noticed that plaster was loose and flaking on some of the walls. He produced the following for the headteacher:

Q B PAINT SERVICES

ESTIMATE FOR PAINTING ROOMS G1, G2, G3 & G4

Remove loose plaster in Rooms G1 & G2 and replace	£550
Paint 4 rooms	£2,000
TOTAL	£2,550

The price seemed reasonable and was cheaper than another they had had, so an order was placed referencing the estimate and the work was carried out.

When the work was completed the bill arrived for £3,000 and the paint was not the high quality finish the school had wanted. What had gone wrong?

First the painter, not unreasonably, was unsure of the amount of work involved in replastering until he began the task, so he had only provided an estimate, ie an approximate cost of what he thought it was likely to be. Second, he had been aware that cost would be an important factor when the school considered who to give the work to, so he had decided to use a cheap brand of paint to save money.

Considering that the work took longer than he had originally expected his final price was not unreasonable. The order had only referenced his estimate and not specified a particular type of paint (we will look at orders later in this chapter) so the school had to pay up.

The lesson is that an estimate is *not an exact price*, only what the supplier thinks it is likely to be. Also, any materials should be specified in detail. If you accept an estimate you must be aware of the possible consequences. If you word an order carefully you can avoid some of the problems, such as being given the wrong materials.

Quotes

Unlike an estimate, a quote is an *exact price* for something. If a supplier gives you a quote you can expect that the price you pay will be the price quoted – provided that the specification is the same. So be sure that the exact specification of the work and materials is on the quote and that it is what you require.

Asking for quotes and estimates

Unless there are special reasons why you do not want to, you should ask for more than one quote or estimate so you can compare prices. But be sure you are comparing like with like, specify exactly what you are asking for and make sure the reply is to that specification. When considering the replies you may also take into account the quality of service and other factors we discussed in the last chapter.

It is also only fair to inform your suppliers that you are asking for other quotes or estimates. If they do not believe they can win on price this gives them the opportunity to specify the service they will give, or choose not to quote on this occasion. That is not unusual, and you should not think a supplier unreasonable if they decide not to quote sometimes.

Tenders

It is normal for LEAs and governors to specify that expenditure above a certain amount should be the subject of competitive tenders. A tender means a formal written offer given in a specified format on the basis of a detailed written description or specification for goods or services.

It may have similarities to a quote, but is usually associated with larger sums of money and more complex projects. Typical examples where tenders will be requested are for cleaning services or building refurbishment. A document replying to a request to tender will describe the goods or services to be provided as well as the price. It may also include other supporting information such as the experience of the company tendering.

There are usually strict guidelines laid down as to how tenders can be called for and how they must be dealt with. With the exception of certain small schools cleaning and maintenance work is normally the subject of compulsory competitive tendering (CCT). (Schools are still able to carry out emergency repairs without the need to go to tender.) The governors and senior management team must make themselves aware of the regulations for tendering. It is normally sensible to seek the advice of an LEA officer when tenders are being planned.

Orders and contracts

When asking a supplier to provide goods or services there must be a written document requesting these. This could be in the form of an order or a contract.

Orders

Orders are normally raised for straightforward purchases. Examples include:

- pupils' books
- new classroom equipment
- a one-off training session being given to staff by an adviser.

The school or LEA will normally have standard order forms which should be used for this purpose. They should be numbered and contain any standard terms and conditions of supply. If you do not have such forms, the LEA should be asked for advice. If a requirement is urgent and so a verbal order is necessary, it must be followed up with a written confirmation. In this case make sure that you put on the order '*Confirmation of verbal order of xxx (date)*', otherwise you may get the order fulfilled twice.

On the order you must be sure to specify *exactly* what you require. This should include such items as:

- detailed description of the item (reference number if available, or name)
- brand
- colour or particular finish, size or other variables
- quantity
- compatibility requirements (eg 'should work with XYZ computer')

- delivery address
- delivery date
- price.

Rule off after the last item on the form and make sure a copy is kept for reference (most standard LEA forms have copies attached). The order should be signed by an individual authorized by the governing body.

This order is then the basis of a contract between yourself and the supplier. If for any reason the supplier cannot supply to the details you give he or she should inform you. If the goods received do not match the order you have a right to reject them. Under normal situations a good supplier will talk to the customer if the order cannot be supplied exactly, and you then have a chance to accept an alternative, delay delivery or go elsewhere. This is the value of a good relationship with suppliers: if the required goods are not in stock they will have a good idea of whether or not you are likely to want an alternative, and what specification it should be. If you have specified a set of textbooks that are an essential part of the curriculum, you are not likely to want an alternative; if you have ordered exercise books with grey covers you may be prepared to accept blue ones.

Contracts

In the past the term 'contract' was understood to mean the terms for employing teaching staff. There have always been other forms of contract, such as for cleaning, building maintenance, school meals and refuse removal, but in the past the LEA was responsible for these. Many of these 'defined activities' are now subject to competitive tendering and the winning supplier is awarded the contract for this work by the school or LEA.

Contracting can be a complex matter, and once the contract is signed the parties are bound legally to the terms of the contract, including the circumstances under which it can be cancelled or curtailed. Therefore it is important that care should be taken when schools are considering entering into contracts and they would be sensible to seek advice. If the school is bound by the terms of a contract and chooses to replace the contractor who had won in competition with another contractor to carry out the same work, or seeks to vary the price or other terms of the contract, then the school will be liable for any costs incurred for breach of contract. The LEA can provide advice on every aspect of contracting – from drawing up specifications, tendering, planning, and health and safety issues. Maximum and minimum times for the length of contracts are usually laid down by the LEA and this should also be checked.

Payment procedures

The school must have a system for checking the goods when they are received to ensure that they match the specification on the order. If they are satisfactory the order or delivery note can then be signed off by the member of staff who required the goods and passed on to the responsible person to be held ready for marrying up with the invoice when it is received. The simple form below is an example of paperwork to support this process. The first part is signed when the goods are received, the second part is signed when the invoice is received.

Form: IC/95

GREAT LONDON SCHOOL INVOICE CERTIFICATION

HEAD OF DEPARTMENT to sign on receipt when goods checked & in good condition

SIGNED ——————————————————————

PRINT NAME ————————————— DATE ————

Order number———————————————————

Invoice arithmetically correct?————————————

Certified correct to charge budget —————————

SIGNED (HEAD TEACHER) ——————————————

PRINT NAME ————————————— DATE ————

The flow chart on page 72 shows a procedure for the cycle from purchasing through to payment. Payment should not be made until a proper invoice has been received, checked, coded and certified for payment by confirming:

- the goods have been received and are correct;
- the cost matched the order;
- payment has not already been made;
- the VAT has been correctly treated;
- copy orders have been endorsed;
- discounts where agreed have been given.

When payment has been made the invoices should be marked 'Paid' and stored securely in order.

Invoices

Invoices should be certified by an approved member of staff who is different from the individual who signed the order and checked the goods.

The invoice must be an original, not photocopied, and should state:

- goods supplied
- order number
- discounts given (if applicable)
- VAT (if applicable) as a separate item
- payment terms
- payment address.

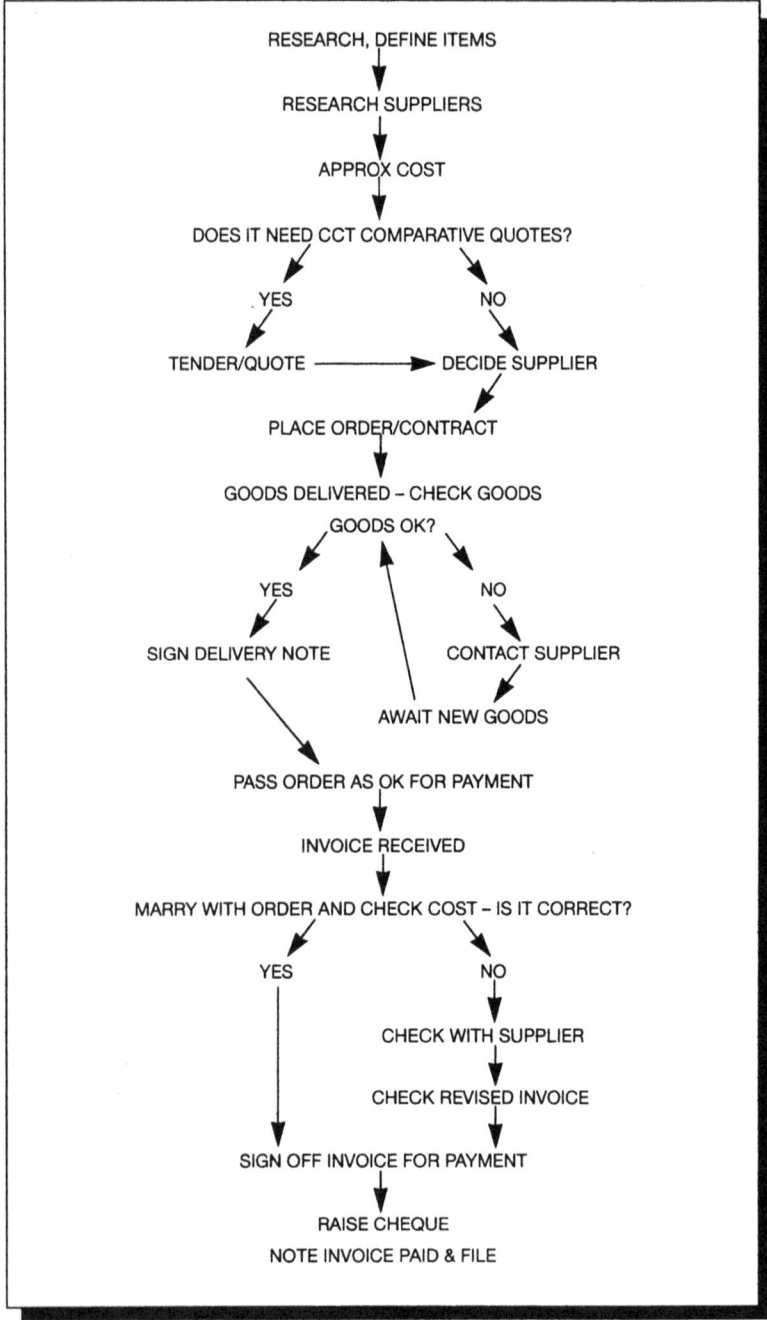

ACTIVITY

Find out what procedure and forms are used in your school. Compare them with the procedure in the flow chart. If they are different:

- Can you improve the school's process?
- If so – how?
- Arrange to discuss your ideas for improvements with a senior colleague.

Summary

Quotes are exact prices, estimates are not. Make sure you know exactly what you are ordering and specify accurately and in detail.

For purchases use official order forms where these are available and state the conditions of purchase if this is not already printed on the form.

Consider lease or rent if this is more suitable to the product than outright purchase.

Use the tendering procedure for large purchases (use local guidelines for the minimum amount).

Have a robust procedure for checking receipt of goods on delivery and correct amounts on invoices. Only pay when you are satisfied these are correct.

CHAPTER 7
Cost Control

Keeping a check on progress

Once a budget has been set the progress of the finances must be monitored and controlled. As stated before, this is both a legal requirement, and makes good management sense. The figure below illustrates the matching of management and financial roles.

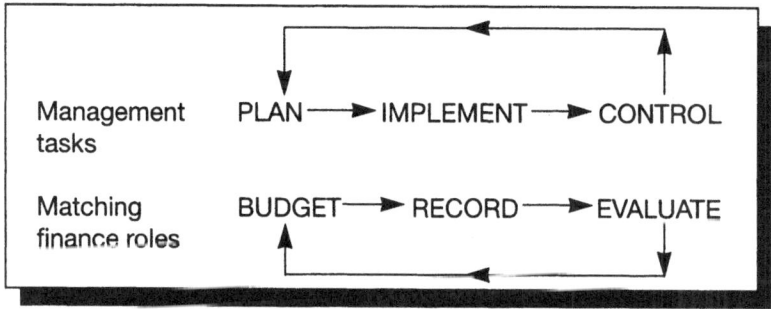

If you are setting out on a journey to somewhere new you plan your route beforehand. Then, as you travel, you check your progress on the way by looking at road signs and comparing these with your map or plan. In this way you can keep a check on your progress, so if you are going off route you can correct your mistake before you go too far. Controlling finances can be thought of as a similar routine: if you check your expenditure against budget at regular intervals you will not go too far off course before you see the problem and take steps to bring your finances back into line. To do this effectively you will need a system.

Different schools will have different systems for processing and recording financial information and transactions. This could include purchasing, payroll and systems for collecting income. To enable them to make informed decisions, governors and headteachers will need to rely on the information which these systems provide. Therefore it is essential that the information provided is as accurate as possible.

Before we go on to consider control systems we will look at some more financial terminology. In the following sections we will explain *creditors, cash management* and *variance analysis*, as well as looking at ways of generating income.

Creditors

Creditors are people to whom we owe money. This includes *all* the money we owe, whether it be thousands of pounds for a major contract or a few pounds for some pencils. In company accounts the total of creditors is deducted from the working capital the company has. This gives the 'net working capital'. In schools you should do the same – take away any money you owe from the money you have to find out what you have got left to spend. Remember to include everything:

- trade creditors – payments outstanding on purchases;
- taxation – any VAT or other taxes you may owe;
- loans – payments owed to banks for short-term borrowings.

Some organizations help their cash flow by not paying their creditors promptly, but this can be counterproductive. It is easier to gain advantageous prices when you can offer prompt payment. Customers who pay late will gain a reputation with suppliers and will find themselves being quoted higher prices. Small businesses in particular need good cash flow to keep them going; too many bad payers and they could even go out of business.

Cash management

In a company 'cash' means money to which it has easy access, ie money in the bank and short term investments which it can easily turn into cash. In schools this could also include money held by the LEA on behalf of the school but which it has not yet drawn down into its own accounts.

Managing this money is important for three main reasons:

1. It is needed for transactions to meet everyday payments to employees and creditors.
2. It is advisable to hold a 'buffer' against unexpected cash needs.
3. It can help with the negotiation of good prices by enabling the school to offer prompt payment.

Investment

However, the advantage of holding cash needs to be balanced against the ability to earn profit from money not being used, ie by investing the money. As you will know from personal experience, the longer the money is invested the greater the return. For example current bank accounts are totally flexible, but pay little or no interest; deposit accounts and building society accounts pay interest on an increasing scale depending on the amount invested and the period of investment. Therefore, a school should consider what its long- and short-term needs are, and decide how much money it can invest for what period. Idle cash does not earn anything.

Making money

The generation of income is not a primary part of the school's function; it should not detract from the main purpose of the school. However, as we described in Chapter 1, there are certain approved ways in which a school can generate income, such as letting of rooms, and these should be considered.

Any activities for financial gain should be approved by the governing body and carefully monitored and controlled. They must be accounted for in the school's accounts and tax paid on profits. Schools should seek advice on what they are allowed to undertake in this area from their LEA Finance Department.

Controlling costs

One way to make money is by not spending too much! This sounds perfectly obvious, but it is advice often ignored or misunderstood.

Obviously you will want to spend money on books, equipment and other items directly related to improving your pupils' learning. Maintenance, energy bills and other services are necessary and, although you may not want to, they also have to be paid for. However, there are things which you pay for which you may not want or need – these are the things that can be controlled and enable you to save money.

In Chapter 2 we described various basic financial concepts – fixed and variable costs, direct and indirect costs. We also described overheads – the costs which are part of running the school, but not related directly to the provision of learning for the pupils. In most of these areas savings can be made.

- Certain items (eg cleaning and maintenance) are essential, but the costs can be controlled by the placement of contracts with cost-effective suppliers.
- Items such as light and heating can be controlled by ensuring that there is no waste.
- Items such as stationery can be controlled by careful monitoring of their use.

The school's financial managers should encourage all staff and pupils to reduce waste and control expenditure wherever this will not diminish the educational value of what the school does. In this way there will be more money available for the important parts of the budget which improve the service to the pupils.

Measuring performance against budget – variance analysis

The budget is the start point of your control system. Let's look back at a detail of the Geography Department budget shown in Chapter 3.

GEOGRAPHY DEPARTMENT BUDGET FOR 1995–96

ITEM	BUDGET	ACTUAL
Set atlases for year 10 30 x £9	£ 270	£ 300
Set 'Europe' textbooks for year 12	£ 360	£ 390

From this we can see that the actual spend is £60 over budget. This is the *variance*. The variance is the difference between what you planned, or budgeted for, and what you actually spent. A positive or favourable variance is when you underspend (ie save money) so there is more money available than you anticipated. An adverse, unfavourable or negative variance is when you overspend, so your financial position is worse than you anticipated.

The same part of the departmental budget would appear on a spreadsheet, with the variance shown, as:

GEOGRAPHY DEPARTMENT BUDGET FOR 1995–96

ITEM	BUDGET	ACTUAL	VAR
Set atlases for year 10 30 x £9	£270	£300	£(30)
Set 'Europe' textbooks for year 12	£360	£390	£(30)

By keeping a simple record of every transaction as it occurs you can check your progress against plan. By variance analysis we can understand the reasons why actual performance differs from planned performance.

ACTIVITY

If the information shown above is to be held on a spreadsheet, at what stage should the spreadsheet be completed? Look back at the flow charts in Chapters 3 and 6 to help you decide at which point the details above should be completed.

If the spreadsheet like the one above is completed at the quote stage, the teacher can decide whether or not to go ahead with these purchases or look for an alternative, cheaper, item. If the spreadsheet is not completed until the invoice comes in then the money is already committed, and savings will *have* to be made on the other items not yet purchased.

It is therefore a good idea to get estimates as accurate as possible at your budget stage. Then complete the spreadsheet when you have actual quotes to compare budget with actual. The process for checking costs could look like this:

STAGE	ACTION
Budget	Decide on requirements Get estimate Add 'contingency' to budget
Purchasing	Get quote Compare quote and budget Decide on purchase
Receipt of invoice	Finally complete spreadsheet Add variance (if any) to total
Before next purchase	Compare budget with actual and consider surplus/deficit available for spend

The variances shown above are simple, and the reasons quite obvious. When considering the whole school budget it is more complex. It needs to take account of income as well as expenditure and the overall variances should be considered as well as the individual items. The headteacher or financial manager should ask each department or area that produces a budget to describe its variances and provide an explanation. This can be considered as part of the whole school's financial performance.

Bench-marking

Another way of reviewing departmental budget results is through a 'bench-marking' process, whereby results are compared against equivalent costs in other schools well known for their efficient and effective financial practices. By sharing information and ideas both parties can learn from the exercise.

Planning for contingencies

By delegating responsibility for financial affairs to schools, the LEAs' flexibility to cope with unexpected additional costs has been greatly reduced. It is normal for LEAs to retain some funds to help cope with emergencies and unexpected changes. This is likely to cover such items as:

● significant variations in pupil numbers;
● errors which arise from its application of the funding formula;
● fire or severe acts of vandalism;
● certain types of loss or theft.

There is therefore some additional money available for schools under these exceptional circumstances. But these funds are limited and they will not cover deficits caused by internal bad planning or mismanagement, neither will they cover items which would normally be bought by the school but which it had failed to budget for. It is sensible then that within the budget some allowance is made for the unexpected.

ACTIVITY

Make a list of any expenditure which your department or school has had to or wanted to make in the last financial year, but was not in the budget. Ask colleagues if you do not have this information yourself.

Why did these changes occur? Consider ways of improving the planning process in the future.

The items you have listed were omitted either because they were not carefully thought out, or were items which could not have been realistically predicted and so might have been covered in a contingency allowance. In departmental budgets contingency allowance should include:

1. a percentage for price rises (especially for items to be purchased some time in the future);
2. an allowance for repairs and maintenance of equipment;
3. an allowance for additional books if class sizes rise;
4. allowances for new books and materials for changes in the curriculum.

(You may think of others you can add to this list.)

Within the whole school budget other items should be covered, overall allowances for situations in the list above plus items such as increases in telephone bills and rises in fuel and utility costs.

Setting up a control system

In Chapter 6 we looked at a simple system for checking purchases, orders and invoices. To control the total finances a similar but more complex system can be used.

When building internal financial controls into the system, schools must be confident that all transactions will be properly processed and that errors will be detected promptly. These could include:

- internal checking – one person's work being checked by another;
- separation of duties so that key tasks are given to different members of staff (as in our process in Chapter 6 – orders are raised and goods checked by one person, invoices checked by another);
- certain transactions must be authorized by a second person – such as expenditure over a given amount, signing cheques or the payment of invoices;
- manuals and guidelines must be produced so everyone involved is clear about their duties and responsibilities as well as exactly how to carry out tasks.

We can now add three additional steps to the planning process we considered in Chapter 3.

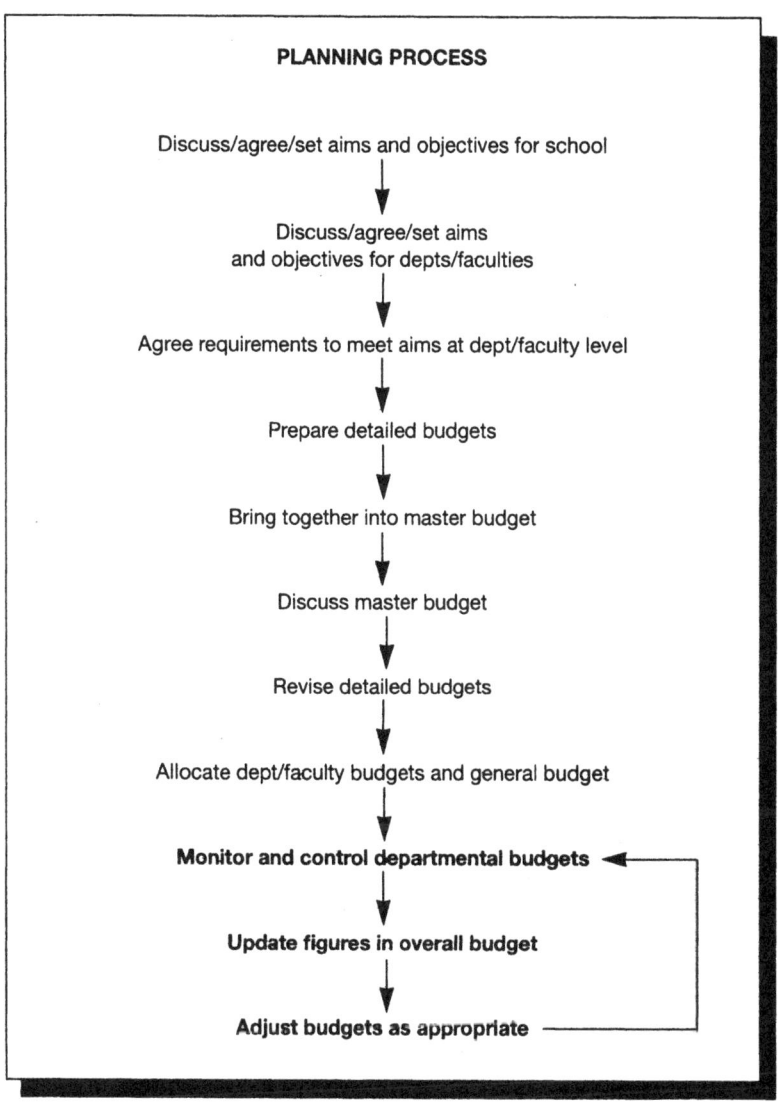

PLANNING PROCESS

Discuss/agree/set aims and objectives for school

↓

Discuss/agree/set aims
and objectives for depts/faculties

↓

Agree requirements to meet aims at dept/faculty level

↓

Prepare detailed budgets

↓

Bring together into master budget

↓

Discuss master budget

↓

Revise detailed budgets

↓

Allocate dept/faculty budgets and general budget

↓

Monitor and control departmental budgets ←

↓

Update figures in overall budget

↓

Adjust budgets as appropriate

The monitoring procedures for departments and the school as a whole should include a system for:

1. filing orders awaiting delivery so they are checked at regular intervals and chased if necessary;

2. filing invoices to be paid so they will be paid on the due date and not forgotten.

The monitoring and control should take place on a regular basis. With departmental budgets and the general budget it should be done *every time* a transaction takes place (when an order is raised, when an invoice is received). The overall budget should be monitored on a time-based system, weekly in large schools with many transactions, less often in smaller schools, but certainly on a monthly basis. LEAs will have a system for reporting financial information, usually on a monthly basis, and this may be used to trigger your own checking procedure.

Non-standard situations

The system of comparing expenditure with budget and adjusting plans accordingly will work well for normal situations if it is adhered to and updated regularly. There may, however, be abnormal situations which need to be catered for. Such situations could include:

- when someone has not paid you money they owe;
- when an invoice is overpriced;
- when goods fail to arrive.

In each case the first step is to talk to the supplier or customer concerned. There may be a perfectly simple explanation and the situation can be easily resolved. If it cannot be resolved to your satisfaction, take all the details to the school's financial manager and ask for advice. If he or she cannot deal with it, they can go to the headteacher, governors or LEA for further advice. It is *essential*, though, in these situations, that you have everything well documented and available for scrutiny.

ACTIVITY

Using the guidelines above, draw a flow chart of your own system as it exists now. If you do not know what it is, you should use this opportunity to find out. If your school or department does not have a documented system, then think about the financial transactions you may have to make. Look again at our guidelines and draw up a system for yourself.

You may like to use this as the basis for discussion with colleagues to begin to develop a formal system for your school.

Forms

To enable you to record the financial information you need there are certain conventional records as we discussed in Chapter 4. But to record your own day-to-day transactions you may want to develop your own records. Most LEAs have standard reporting procedures for receiving a school's financial information. If you have to complete forms for the LEA then it is sensible to use internal records which are compatible.

Some records will need to be presented in such a way that the data can easily be input on to the LEA's or school's computerized financial system. Often this is not flexible enough to take account of all the idiosyncrasies of each school, so you may have to adapt your preferred method to make the best use of the computerized records.

If you are going to use forms to keep records:

1. Check the LEA requirements and see if they have standard forms.
2. Check the school's requirements and see if they have standard forms.

If you are not constrained in this way then you should produce your own forms – but remember these rules of forms design:

Forms design checklist

Only produce a form if it is necessary and useful.

Only include necessary information.

Remember to include *all* necessary information.

Make it clear – so others can understand it as well as the designer.

Look at the form below.

Item	Estimate	Budget	Actual
Total for year			
Checked by:		**Date:**	

What is wrong with the form? What is there is useful, but it does not give the whole picture. It does not have space for:

- school name
- department or subject name
- start and finish dates
- when it is checked there should be space to print and sign – which does it require?

So it is not much use to anyone needing the information except the originator – and he or she may not be available when needed.

ACTIVITY

Make a list of any forms you think would be useful to your financial records. Find out if the LEA or school has forms for this. If so, obtain copies. If not, use the guidelines above to design your own form. When it is designed take it to a colleague and ask for their opinion:

- Is it clear?
- Is it useful?
- Is it necessary?

If the response to all three is 'Yes', then use the form for a month or a term, and see how useful it is to you. If necessary, revise it to suit your needs.

Summary

Monitoring the financial information will enable you to keep control of the finances.

Managing cash can improve your flexibility in negotiating deals. Money is made by:

- investment
- income-generating schemes

- control of costs
- control of waste.

Analyse budget against actual expenditure, work out the variance and ask 'Why?' Then take steps to learn from mistakes and budget more accurately in future.

Set up a robust control system. Keep it simple with clear, straightforward paperwork. Make sure everyone knows why it is there and how to use it. Ensure that everyone uses it properly.

References

Croner's – *School Governor's Manual*

Local Education Authority – *LMS Handbook or Guide*
There should be one available for every LEA and there will be a book/binder/section dealing with finance.

Audit Commission – *Keeping Your Balance*, produced by OFSTED

Useful Addresses

Croner Publications Ltd
London Road
Kingston upon Thames
Surrey, KT2 6SR

OFSTED
Office for Standards in Education
Alexandra House
29–33 Kingsway
London, WC2B 6SE

VAT Central Unit
Alexander House
Victoria Avenue
Southend-on-Sea
Essex, SS99 1AA

Glossary Of Terms

Accounts   A systematic record of money spent and received.

Audit   Official examination of accounts to see they are in order.

Balance sheet   A statement of the financial position (assets, liabilities and capital) of an organization at a particular point in time.

Budget   The forecast of what you expect to spend.

Capital expenditure   Expenditure on fixed assets.

Controllable costs   Costs which can be controlled by the organization and staff.

Cost centre   An administrative division rather like a cash box. Everything which that area spends is charged to that area and the money is taken out of its cash supply.

Credit   Income or money owed by us to others.

Creditors   Those to whom we owe money.

Debit   Money spent or owed to us.

Debtors   Those who owe money to us or our school/business. The amount is the debt.

Depreciable amount   The amount of value lost during the useful life of an item.

Depreciation   The way in which the reduction in the fixed value of an item is shown in the accounts.

Direct costs   Costs which are directly related to making any product or providing a service, eg wages of labour working on the product or raw material costs.

Estimate   An approximate price of what something is expected to cost.

Fixed assets   Items purchased and owned by the business. They represent the means by which an organization earns its profits and they are for repeated use over a number of years. We call them 'fixed' because they are not for sale in the course of everyday business. They include items such as land, buildings, plant and machinery, office equipment, and computers.

Fixed costs   Costs such as rates, insurance and depreciation which are not affected by services provided or production.

Indirect costs   Costs not directly related to making the product or giving the service, eg people to provide back-up for the direct labour such as staff to pay wages, and the costs of running the offices.

Liability   The sum we are liable to pay (ie the credit balance).

Non-controllable costs   Costs which are beyond the control of the organization such as rates and fixed charges.

Overheads   Costs essential to running the organization. They may or may not be directly related to the provision of the product or service.

Profit   Revenue minus costs, or the amount left over from the sale of goods after you have taken out all your expenditure.

Quote   Exact price which will be charged for specified goods or services.

Residual value   The amount of money which any fixed asset is worth after it has been depreciated.

Revenue   The money that the organization receives. It is not the same as what the customer pays because the full price may include other items such as taxes.

Spreadsheet   A 'spread' of all the financial information about a department/organization showing income, expenditure and balances.

Tender   Formal offer of the provision of specified goods or services for a given price.

Variable costs   Costs which can change at different times, eg as production volume or number of services provided changes.

Variance   Difference between planned and actual spending. It may be positive or negative.